Good News and Bad News

About the Judgment

Morris L. Venden

Pacific Press Publishing Association
Mountain View, California
Oshawa, Ontario

Copyright © 1982 by
Pacific Press Publishing Association
Printed in United States of America

Reprinted 1983

Library of Congress Cataloging in Publication Data

Venden, Morris L.
   Good news and bad news about the Judgment.
   (Harvest)
   1. Seventh-day Adventists—Doctrinal and contro-
versial works. I. Title.
BX6154.V43 236'.9 82-7863
ISBN 0-8163-0484-X AACR2

Contents

Don't Read This Book If . . .

Don't read this book if you want a scholarly exegesis on the prophecies of Daniel and Revelation. If you're looking for some input on interpreting the intricacies of Hebrews, for help in translating the Greek text, or for directions for making your own scale-model sanctuary, then you'd better look elsewhere.

The dialogue concerning the investigative judgment and related topics within our church today seems primarily an attempt to settle on our beliefs concerning sin and righteousness and salvation. The investigative judgment, as a historical and eschatological event, is not really threatening. What scares many of us Adventists is wondering how it relates to sin and righteousness. We're not sure that our belief in salvation by faith in Jesus Christ alone can hold up to a full-fledged judgment scene, complete with books of angel records for every thought, word and deed. The idea of having our lives investigated isn't too encouraging, and our assurance of salvation pales at the possibility of having our names blotted out in the book of life.

It's not our lack of understanding of how Daniel 8 relates to Leviticus 16 that causes the sleepless nights. It's our lack of understanding of how the apparent bad news of the judgment relates to the good news of the gospel. Lurking behind all of the theological questions about this pillar of our faith is the yet unanswered question to many minds: Suppose the scholars would prove beyond a shadow of a doubt that the investigative judgment is indeed Bible truth—what then?

The premise of this book is that the sanctuary and judgment truths are impossible to understand aright unless we understand the gospel correctly. And yet the gospel is understood clearly only when we have a correct understanding of the sanctuary and judgment. The two truths stand or fall together. Those today who are abandoning their belief about the judgment will discover ultimately that they must abandon the gospel as well. The news about the judgment and the news of the gospel are both equally good and equally bad. Perhaps when we come to understand the *bad* news of the gospel, we will be better equipped to understand the *good* news of the judgment.

If you are interested in the belief and experience of salvation by faith in Jesus alone, but you are equally interested in continuing to accept the unique pillars of our faith, then I invite you to a careful study of the relationship between these subjects. Keep reading, for I have some good news for you! But first, the bad.

The Bad News of the Gospel

How would you feel if the first thing you discovered upon reaching heaven was that H. M. S. Richards was missing? And what if you then found out that your next-door neighbor was Adolph Hitler? Or what if you looked in vain for your son or daughter who had been heavily involved in the drug scene, and then discovered that the one who had sold them the dope was living across the street?

Now I am not campaigning for any of these! But we do know that there will be some big surprises in heaven. People we thought would surely be there may be missing, and some we thought surely wouldn't be there may be present. God judges by a different system from ours, for we look only at the outward appearance, but God looks on the heart.

As we try to understand a little more about God's system, let's look at Matthew 20:1-16. It's one of the strangest stories Jesus ever told. And it brings us face-to-face with the bad news of the gospel.

"For the kingdom of heaven is like unto a man that is an householder, which went out early in the morning to hire labourers into his vineyard. And when he had agreed with the labourers for a penny a day, he sent them into his vineyard.

7

"And he went out about the third hour [9:00 a.m.], and saw others standing idle in the marketplace, and said unto them: Go ye also into the vineyard, and whatsoever is right I will give you. And they went their way." Verses 1-4. They didn't have an agreed sum of payment; they accepted his offer of "whatsoever is right." They trusted him.

Verses 5-7: "Again he went out about the sixth and ninth hour, and did likewise. And about the eleventh hour he went out, and found others standing idle, and saith unto them, Why stand ye here all the day idle? They say unto him, Because no man hath hired us. He saith unto them, Go ye also into the vineyard; and whatsoever is right, that shall ye receive."

Well, a worker can't lose at 5:00 p.m. with only one hour before time to quit. If all he does is stuff himself with grapes during the last hour and get nothing for his labor, he is still better off than he would be just standing on the street corner. These workers who were hired the last hour were fresh. They had done nothing all day. Can't you see them picking grapes faster than anybody else, just for the novelty of having something to do besides standing around? And perhaps the rest of the workers sniffed and said, "Sure, they're full of pep. Wait till they've worked for twelve hours like we have, and then see what happens to their enthusiasm." And finally it was quitting time.

The vineyard owner is a troublemaker

But now the plot thickens. Verse 8: "So when the even was come, the lord of the vineyard saith unto his steward, Call the labourers, and give them their hire, beginning from the last unto the first."

Here was the first sign of trouble. These people had gotten up before sunrise, eaten a hurried breakfast, and walked down to the corner on Main Street where those blue buses with the dingy windows pick them up and take them to the vineyard. They had been working for twelve hours. They were hot and dusty. They were tired and anxious to get home, shower, have something to eat, pay a little attention to the kiddies, and go to sleep reading the evening paper. They would fall into bed exhausted, only to do it all over again tomorrow. And now, instead of getting their pay and being allowed to go on their way, they had to stand there and wait for the miserable one-hour workers to get paid first. Now don't you agree with me that the vineyard owner is a troublemaker?

Then the Bible says, "And when they came that were hired about the eleventh hour, they received every man a penny [a day's wage]." Verse 9.

Suddenly things began to look good. It looked good for the eleventh-hour workers, who received a whole day's pay for one hour's work. There are two extremes of reactions you could have if you were in their place. One reaction could be to figure that the vineyard owner was a soft touch and plan how you could rip him off the next day. Second, an opposite reaction would be to be so grateful for the generosity of the kind vineyard owner that you resolve to come out and work the following day for free!

But not only did things look good to the one-hour workers. Things looked good to the twelve-hour workers as well. They looked over the shoulders of the ones who were paid first, whipped out their pocket calculators, and figured that vacation time had arrived at last! In their minds they were already home announcing the good news to the family, getting out the Coleman stove and the pup tents, and packing the station wagon. They were impressed with the generosity of the vineyard owner.

They didn't stay impressed. Verse 10: "But when the first came, they supposed that they should have received more; and they likewise received every man a penny." Now is this good news or bad news?

If the vineyard owner had chosen to pay the twelve-hour workers first and sent them on their way, then they may not have discovered what he paid the other workers. But for some reason this vineyard owner *wanted* them to see. He was a troublemaker.

In that case, just keep your money!

When the twelve-hour workers saw that their vacation plans had to be cancelled, they were upset. It says, "And when they had received it, they murmured against the goodman of the house, saying, These last have wrought but one hour, and thou hast made them equal unto us, which have borne the burden and heat of the day. But he answered one of them, and said, Friend, I do thee no wrong: didst not thou agree with me for a penny? Take that thine is, and go thy way: I will give unto this last, even as unto thee. Is it not lawful for me to do what I will with mine own? Is thine eye evil, because I am good? So the last shall be first, and the first last: for many be called, but few chosen." Verses 11-16.

"Take that thine is, and go thy way." Apparently they didn't even want to take their pay. They were ready to tell the vineyard owner he could just keep his filthy money. He had to plead with them to take it with them. Now don't you agree that this vineyard owner is a troublemaker?

If you don't think the vineyard owner was trying to make trouble, maybe you have some idea of who the vineyard owner is! And if he is God, you don't want to admit that sometimes God's system looks strange to us, for the system of the world we are used to is entirely different. Even the spiritually mature, who have learned to appreciate God's system as far as heavenly things are concerned, must still live by the merit system in temporal matters. In our work, in our schools, in our lives here on earth, everything is based on the system of merit. You get what you earn, and you earn what you get. No more, and hopefully no less. It has permeated all of society. It has permeated the church. From the cradle on up, every one of us have had to live with the system of merit.

Gifts aren't fair

To receive a gift, really and truly for free, is a rare thing in this world, and may even make the receiver uncomfortable. Even the lotteries and sweepstakes have to go to a great deal of trouble to prove to everybody that it is chance that picks the winner—that the winner is nobody's favorite. To give prizes or gifts by any method except by random selection isn't considered "fair." And the ones who stand by and watch a gift bestowed upon another—as in, for example, an inheritance situation—are often upset at the unfairness of such an act.

When I was in the first grade, I was going to school in New York City. All year we worked hard on progressive classwork. I was studying to be a Sunbeam and Builder—you know, the vegetarian Boy Scout program. I had worked hard and looked forward eagerly to the night of the investiture service.

When the youth director arrived, he spread out on the table all of the scarves and pins for all of those who were being invested in the various classes. There were the Friend and Companion classes, and the Comrades, and Master Comrades. (That was before we had heard of the Russians!) The scarf for the Master Comrade was a beautiful orange kerchief, with a shiny plastic slider. And all of the classes had plastic sliders, except for the Sunbeams and Builders. For the Sunbeams and Builders, there was only a small, plain, green kerchief, and you had to tie the ends together in a knot to hold it around your neck.

I remember wanting a plastic slider so much that night that I smiled my biggest smiles at that youth director, hoping he would be impressed with me and give me one of those plastic sliders. But there was no way, and when the investiture service was over and done, I had gotten just what I earned, and I had earned just what I got. I had my Builder and Sunbeam buttons and my little green kerchief.

But then someone got a bright idea. My father and uncle were evangelists in town, holding meetings in Carnegie Hall. And someone said, "Why don't we have the evangelists and their wives come up and invest them as Master Comrades! They must know all these requirements."

So they invited my father and mother and uncle and aunt up front and invested them as Master Comrades. They got the plastic sliders and everything! And I knew good and well that my father and mother hadn't gone through the requirements even for Sunbeam and Builder!

I had thought I loved my father and mother, until then. And I still did, I guess. But I wasn't at all sure about that youth director! The whole experience set my interest in progressive classwork back by about twenty years.

I am not worthy

In Luke 7 we read about the centurion's servant who was sick. And at his request, the Jewish rulers came to Jesus asking that his servant be healed. They were still on the merit system. You don't ever find them coming and requesting healing for a blind beggar or a leper or a little widow woman. But the centurian had built them a synagogue. So they came to Jesus, and "they besought him instantly, saying, That he was worthy for whom he should do this: for he loveth our nation, and he hath built us a synagogue." Verses 4, 5.

12

Jesus started out for the centurion's house, and when finally the centurion himself came to Jesus, in spite of the fact that the Jewish leaders thought he was worthy, the centurion said of himself, "I am not worthy." And Jesus marveled at him and said, "I have not found so great faith, no, not in Israel." Verses 6, 9.

Here's the bad news

It's the fact that none of us can ever be worthy, it's the truth that no one can ever earn or merit God's grace or favor that is the bad news of the gospel. It has been a universal disease of humanity that we want to be worthy. When we have toiled through the heat of the day and then we see those who come at the last minute receiving a reward equal to ours, we find our reward hard to take. The message that we can never be saved in any way on the basis of our own works can be bad news to the one who is used to paying his entire way. Yet it is the foundation of God's economy. He is on the gift system all the way.

You are called to the bedside of a dying missionary. The elders have come to anoint him. And you remind the Lord of all of his years of faithful service—how he buried a son or daughter, perhaps a wife, out there in the far-flung fields. You remind the Lord of all that he could yet do in His work. And you don't *quite* say it, but it's there, in the background, "Lord, this man really deserves Your help." And the missionary dies, and you go on your way, wondering about God's system of working.

Then you go to the bedside of a backslider. He's dying in a hospital of a heart attack. There's scarcely enough blood pumping across his brain to enable him to think. Between gasps he says, "Preacher, I'm a backslider. I've treated God badly for years. But please pray for me that I'll come up in the right resurrection." There are no elders and no oil. You don't even ask that he be healed. You just ask that he come up in the right resurrection. And he's healed and walks out of the hospital with a heart apparently as good as anybody's. And you go your way, pondering God's system.

God's free grace may be good news for a dying back-slider—but what about the dying missionary? Doesn't he deserve at least equal treatment? Doesn't he *de-serve–?*

And we continue to be astonished at God's way of working.

The extra reward for the twelve-hour workers

In order to understand why God's system is good news for the twelve-hour workers, for the dying missionary, as well as for the latecomers, we need to back up to Matthew 19. A rich man had come to Jesus asking what to do to enter into life. Jesus told him to sell all he had, give to the poor, and come and follow Him. The rich man went away sorrowful, for he had great possessions. Verses 16-22.

The disciples watched it happen, and one of them managed to have enough courage to ask what all of them were thinking: "Lord, this rich man went away because he had great possessions, and he wasn't willing to give them up. However, we're still here. We haven't gone away, and we have left all to follow You. What are we going to get?" See verse 27.

If you had been in Jesus' shoes at this juncture, you could easily have gotten discouraged. He had been working with these men for almost three years, trying to teach them the values of the kingdom. If it had been one of us, we might easily have said, "You men are hopeless. Give me another twelve. I'm starting over." But Jesus was patient, and He met them where they were. He said, "In the kingdom, there are going to be twelve thrones, and you will each have a throne, and

14

will judge the twelve tribes of Israel." See verse 28. And you can see Peter and the other disciples standing a little taller as they begin to picture the scene!

But then Jesus makes a very interesting statement that we wouldn't want to miss. "Every one that hath forsaken houses, or brethren, or sisters, or father, or mother, or wife, or children, or lands, for my name's sake, shall receive an hundredfold" (verse 29), and Mark adds, "Now in this time, . . . and in the world to come eternal life" (Mark 10:30). Please notice the two rewards. Those who have forsaken all and followed Jesus will receive an hundredfold. When? Now. At this present time. And the other reward is eternal life at the end of the age when Jesus comes again.

So there are two rewards. And with that in mind, we can return to the vineyard and understand the rest of the story. There is a reward of being able to work throughout the day with the kind vineyard owner. It is rewarding to become involved in service and meaningful work for the entire day. It is not necessary to wait for the end of the day for the reward—the reward comes all through the day.

If you know a vital relationship with Jesus, if you know God as it is your privilege to know Him, then your primary focus is not on the reward at the end of the day. Your primary focus is the joy of fellowship and service with Him right now. Isn't that true? These one-hour workers, who spent the day out on the street corner, are they the winners or the losers? It's *boring* out there! But the vineyard is an exciting place. And unless you are merely putting in your time, trying hard to make it to heaven, you can easily understand this. If you don't know the thrill of entering into relationship and service with the Lord Jesus today, then you are miserable now, and you'll be miserable at the end too.

The happiest person today is the one who is the

15

most involved in service to others, and the most miserable person today is the one who is the most turned in on himself. If your whole focus is on yourself and on trying to make yourself happy, you will be miserable. But when you forget self and reach out to others, you find happiness automatically. The rewards that come with the burden and heat of the day more than compensate for the burden and heat of the day, even if there were no reward at the end.

If God calls you to some hard place of service for Him and you know that He has called you, then the sacrifice is not in going. The sacrifice would be to stay home! And many missionaries can tell you that's true.

Idleness is a real drag

When I was in college, toward the end of one year the pressure had really built up. I was tired. And I told my brother one morning that I wished I could go to bed for a week. That very day, up on the gym field, we were pole-vaulting, and my pole broke. I landed on my head and was knocked unconscious. I got a brain concussion. I also got a strange heart problem called a pericardial friction, rub caused by trauma. The medical students at Loma Linda found it a curiosity to listen to my heartbeat from across the room. And the doctor said, "Go to bed for a week." I loved it—for the first three hours. Then it was terrible.

Have you ever left for a vacation and been so tired that you resolved to do nothing but set up a cot and some mosquito netting, and sleep and read by the lake? And as soon as you arrive at the lake, you hurry to set up the cot, and you crawl under the netting. But after thirty minutes you can't stand it. And soon you're out building a raft to go across the lake or damming up the creek or polishing the hubcaps on your car. In all of life, activity is the only way to survive. And activity is as necessary to the Christian life as to the physical life. It is in working that we stay alive.

Even in heaven, that land of rest, there will still be the joy of service for others. That's what the angels are all about. They have found their joy for thousands of years in ministering to human beings, who are in every way inferior to them.

Can't you imagine it? One day your angel comes by your mansion for a visit. And he says, "How would you like to take a trip?"

And you say, "Sure—count me in. Just wait till I pack."

"No," he says, "there's no need to pack. Nothing to pack!"

You say, "Oh, that's right. Well, let me say goodbye to my friends, and then we can leave."

"They'll be here when you get back," he reminds you. "They'll be here forever!"

And so you are ready to go. You've had opportunity to compare notes with this angel friend of yours. You've found out about the time when he saved you from going over the top of Nevada Falls in Yosemite. You didn't even know you were in danger. You've thanked him for saving you from that head-on collision on the highway. And you're eager to spend more time with him.

"Where are we going?"

"To a little planet on the outer rim of a galaxy, to let them hear the story from human lips of what it's like to be ransomed from a world of sin." You know that angels never felt the joy that our salvation brings, and so you start off on tireless flights to worlds afar, to tell those who haven't heard what it's like to be lost—and found again.

And once more you are involved in the timeless and universal principle that the happiest person is the one who is reaching out to others.

17

I invite you today to the rewards, one hundredfold here and now, of working with this kind, loving, generous vineyard owner. And He also has made provision to take care of the rewards at the end of the day, for everybody, whether they worked all day long or came at the last minute. Won't you join me today in pleading with God to transform our hearts so that we can accept His system and thus be happy with Him in heaven forever? It is as we accept His grace, for free, today, that we are enabled to find that the bad news of the gospel is really good news, after all.

The Bad News About Obedience

Do you ever get tired of sinning? If your answer is No, then there are two options: Either you're not tired of it, or you are no longer sinning. Either way, this chapter is not for you. But if your answer is Yes, then there is news for you—the bad news about obedience—which may provide a tremendous encouragement.

Most of us have been able to accept, at one time or another, the bad news of the gospel, that we cannot earn or merit God's forgiving grace. We have admitted that all of our good works can never purchase salvation. But it's not the good works that have been causing us to lie awake at night, staring at the ceiling. It's the other kind! We read texts like Revelation 3:5 and discover that even though our names may be in the book of life, it's possible that they will be blotted out. We see signs all around that emphasize the nearness of Christ's coming. We see the sin and failure still present in our lives. And we are worried. We know we're not doing that well. And we begin to wonder where obedience fits in with what we've believed about salvation through faith in Jesus Christ alone.

Now I have a solution for you today. It's surefire, guaranteed to work. I have here a button that you can push. If you choose to push this button, you will never fall or fail or sin again—forever. Are you interested? Wait just a minute before you decide, because once you push the button, you can't change your mind. If you push this button, it may cut down on some of your fun. It may change your life-style drastically. Are you sure that you are ready to live without sinning? Are you sure you *want to?*

PUSH FOR VICTORY ▶ ⬤

There have been two responses to this offer as I have made it around the country. One response, "Quick! Show me the button!" The other response, "No way! I'm having too much fun the way I am." Usually there are no in-betweens.

Did you decide to push the button? (It would be interesting to know how many of you actually pushed it!) We know that pushing any button, to say nothing of a paper one, couldn't really solve the problem of sinning. But we are often willing to try anything, just in case.

Have you ever been to a service where you wrote your sins on a little piece of paper and carried it to the front of the church to be burned on a makeshift altar? Have you ever sat down and made out a list of New Year's resolutions? Have you ever made promises never to sin again? If overcoming were that simple, many of us would have become overcomers a long time ago. In fact, even if overcoming were extremely difficult, many of us would have become overcomers long ago, if only we had known for a certainty how to achieve it. But we have not known how it was accomplished and so have continued to try the gimmicks to no avail.

What options are available to you when you see the gap between your performance and God's standard of obedience? Perhaps there was a time when you thought that the solution was simply more water under the bridge. Many young people have the idea that by the time they are twenty, or maybe thirty, that somehow they will have outgrown the sin problem.

But those of us who are over thirty have discovered that we have had to raise the number. Now it's forty, or sixty, or eighty! Righteousness by senility! And today the plot thickens, for signs all around us are not of a nature to give us much assurance of being able to get old enough to stop sinning before Jesus comes again, before the time of probation is up for everyone.

There are signs of Christ's coming today that were prophesied as being the *very last* before Jesus comes again. Ninety years ago, two things were predicted would take place at the very end: (1) The investigative judgment would be shot at, and (2) the spirit of prophecy would be attacked. And, if your eyes are open, you can see these prophecies being fulfilled on every hand. The time is just about up, and we're still not overcomers.

Because of the evidence that Jesus' coming is right upon us, people are getting panicky. One of our biggest temptations is to adjust our theology to match our experience, instead of finding out how to change our experience to match our theology. And in spite of our attempts to hide our real concern, we would have to admit that it isn't so much what Ellen White said about the geological formation of volcanos, for instance, that we're having trouble with. The problem is what she said about sin and righteousness. I don't think that people are so worried about whether she borrowed material from Hanna or Edersheim or Uriah Smith. I think they are worried about what she had to say concerning sin and righteousness.

The nominal Christian world, and by "nominal" we mean "in name only," has met the problem by three teachings: (1) Salvation was guaranteed at the cross. (2) Only believe is all a person has to do. And (3) no one can keep the law anyway. All of these have permeated our own church today. There are heavy forces at work trying to cause us to simply accept the theology of the nominal Christian world. We are urged to join them in proclaiming the investigative judgment to be a farce and the spiritual gift to this church a hoax, and to give up expecting to be overcomers. This is why it is so important for us to understand the mission of the church of the remnant, a mission that goes beyond that of Luther and the other Reformers, that prepares a people for the coming of Jesus.

Satan's original charge was that the law of God could not be obeyed. When man broke the law of God, Satan rejoiced and added another charge—that man could not be forgiven. He had no idea that God would pay the penalty Himself. But Jesus' life and death proved that sinners could be forgiven and that the law of God can be obeyed, not only by Jesus, but also by those who live the life of faith as He did. This twofold message of forgiveness *and obedience* is the heart of the remnant mission during the time of the three angels and is the final work of Christ in heaven. Jesus as our High Priest provides forgiveness for sinners *and power* to obey. These two truths are equally necessary. It is extremely important that the last people of God understand this twofold work of Christ. Otherwise it will be impossible for them to fulfill their mission. Justification by faith—God's work for us—and the righteousness of Christ—which includes God's work in us—are the two themes to be presented to a perishing world.

The major theme of Jesus' own book, the book of Revelation, is overcoming. Victory is the keynote of the message of the entire book. We are reminded again

22

and again of the fact that God's grace includes not only unmerited favor, but *unmerited power* as well.

Paul understood it, for he said in Romans 1:17, "The just shall *live* by faith." Those who have been justified by faith are to live by faith as well. Not only justification comes by faith alone, but in the same way, overcoming comes by faith alone. "As ye have therefore received Christ Jesus the Lord, so walk ye in him." Colossians 2:6. All of salvation is realized through faith in Jesus, and through faith only. It is all a free gift.

Back to the vineyard

Jesus used the analogy of the workers in the vineyard to teach the bad news of the gospel, and we can again join Him in the vineyard to learn of the bad news about obedience.

John 15 is probably one of the most outstanding passages in all Scripture showing us how obedience comes and teaching us that genuine obedience is natural and spontaneous. For obedience is the fruit of faith. The fruits of the Spirit are the fruits of faith. And the fruits of faith develop in our lives in the same way that fruit develops in the vineyard. Development happens when the branches are connected to the vine and abide in the vine. "Abide in me, and I in you. As the branch cannot bear fruit of itself, except it abide in the vine; no more can ye, except ye abide in me. I am the vine, ye are the branches. He that abideth in me, and I in him, the same bringeth forth much fruit: for without me ye can do nothing." John 15:4, 5.

What does the word *abide* mean? If you go through your Bible and do a word study on that word, you'll discover that it means nothing more than "to stay." The two men on the road to Emmaus said to the Stranger, "Abide with us." Stay with us, for it is late in the day. There are two important things in the Christian life. The first is to get with Jesus; the second is to stay with Him. In terms of the vineyard, it is important for the branch to become connected with the vine, but it is equally important that the branch *stay* connected.

Here is one of the problems in the Christian world. People have labored under the delusion that if they got with Jesus at some point in time, everything would be taken care of from then on. They become disappointed when they discover this isn't the case. Nothing is taken care of when we get with Jesus—unless we stay with Him.

And how do we stay with Him? In the same way we got with Him. Connection comes by faith, and faith comes by communication. If you don't communicate with someone, you will not be personally acquainted with him. You will not know him. And if you don't know someone, you will not trust him. It's that simple.

The biggest problem of our church today is that we are not connected to the vine. We are not spending time day by day in communicating with Christ. We are not abiding in Him. And the result is that we find that we are producing little, if any, fruit.

Genuine obedience comes naturally as a result of the continuing relationship with Jesus, just as fruit comes naturally as a result of the branch continuing to be connected to the vine. We recognize that this principle is true for the natural world, and many of us admit that it is also true for the spiritual life. But in spite of our admissions, surveys of church members show that only about one out of every four or five is spending any time at all in personal, daily Bible study and prayer and communication with God.

If you are interested in bearing fruit, answer the following questions: Do you know God? Do you know Him as your personal Friend? Did you spend significant time talking to Him this morning? Or were you too busy with your own plans? Since we understand from this parable of the vine and branches that we, as branches, can do nothing if not connected to Him, then the only legitimate place to put our effort would be in becoming connected with Him.

But this presents us with a problem. Fruit doesn't develop overnight. And we're in a hurry. So when we hear that the entire basis of the Christian life is to come into fellowship with the Lord Jesus and to keep on coming to Him, we say, "That sounds good. I think I'll try that." We try it, and it doesn't work. We still make mistakes and fall and fail and sin. And after a few days or weeks or perhaps months, we scrap the whole business and go back to our gimmicks, back to trying hard to be good enough and hoping against hope that we'll make it.

What do you try after you try relationship?

So what's left? After you've "tried" relationship with Jesus, and it "didn't work," what do you try next? The answer is, Nothing. Because you really may not have tried the relationship with Jesus at all! The relationship with Jesus involves total commitment. It involves giving up on yourself and on the possibility of ever becoming an overcomer apart from Him. It involves resolving to continue to seek Jesus day by day, until He comes again, no matter what happens in your life in the meantime. It involves becoming absolutely locked in on the one principle that God gets top priority in your day, that you invite His control over your life day by day *whether you ever get to heaven or not!*

The purpose of the relationship is not to get us to heaven. The purpose of the relationship is not to bring us victory over our sins. The purpose of the relationship is to know God as it is our privilege to know Him. It is for His own sake that we seek Him day by day, not for *our* sake. And while it is inevitable that

25

those who endure to the end in seeking the continuing relationship with Jesus will be saved and also will be overcomers, this is not the primary reason for continuing to seek the relationship with Jesus.

The devil knows that if he can make us think that the purpose of the relationship is for overcoming, he's got us. When—because of our immaturity—he causes us to sin, he can get us to scrap the relationship on the grounds that it "isn't working." And as soon as he can get us to scrap the relationship *for any reason*, he knows he has got us.

If you have your eyes open, you can see this underlying purpose in all that the devil hits us with. Did you fail today? Might as well give up the relationship, the devil insinuates, and try something else. Are you having trials and sorrows and disappointments? Might as well give up on this relationship bit, he counsels, because it's not working. Are you impatient for the fruits of the Spirit to develop in your life? Better try something else, he suggests, since this relationship thing is working too slowly.

You see, you can't keep a relationship going if your primary motivation is to overcome sins. Even if you *have* been overcoming *and* experiencing the victory that comes as a by-product of looking to Jesus. Any time you turn around, put your attention on yourself, and begin checking yourself for fruit, you are going to fall and fail. It is a spiritual law that when you look to self, you are overcome. But when you look to Jesus, you are an overcomer. And one of the main reasons why it takes so long for the fruit to develop is that we insist on swinging back and forth between two extremes—first looking to Jesus and depending on His power but then checking ourselves to see how we're doing. How many of us have spent our entire Christian lives like children in the garden, pulling up the tiny green shoots every few minutes to see if there's a radish there yet. Misdirected effort!

What do you try after you try relationship? There's nothing else to try. Relationship is the end of trying. And that's why it's bad news. Because there's nothing that you can do to earn or merit your obedience. It is a gift. And that's bad news for the person who has done pretty well, on the outside, part of the time! It's a humbling thing to realize that you are just as incapable of dealing with your present sinning as you are to deal with your sins of the past.

But for all of salvation, the answer is in the vineyard. It's in being connected to the Vine—continuously, unbrokenly, every day. It's in finding your joy in the companionship of the Owner of the vineyard. It's bad news, because you can't deserve any of it. But it's still the best news in the whole wide world!

The Good News About the Judgment

Imagine with me a scene in heaven, way back before the beginning of this world's history. Lucifer has sinned. God calls him in before His throne and destroys him on the spot. The next morning the other angels come around and ask, "Where's Lucifer?"

God says, "He's gone."

The angels say, "What's 'gone' "?

God answers, "I killed him."

"Killed him? What does 'killed' mean?"

"I destroyed him because he sinned."

And the angels say, "Sinned? What's that? What are You talking about?"

God says, "Don't you trust Me?"

And they say, "Well, we did—until now."

There are people today who say that there's no need for an investigative judgment, because the Lord knows those who are His. Of course He does! But if God had wanted to bypass our intelligence, leave our questions unanswered, and have a government based on blind trust, He should have started a long time ago, right? If He had wanted to use that approach, God could have used it way back at the beginning of sin and at least have saved us all the years of pain and misery that sin has brought. But He didn't. He chose to allow sin to demonstrate itself to its ultimate end so that it will never rise again. And He has operated in such a way during the entire great controversy that every one of us can base his trust on an intelligent understanding of His methods.

Who needs the investigative judgment?

Perhaps you remember hearing about the Glacier View meeting, where church administrators and theologians discussed some of the issues connected with the investigative judgment. The Sabbath immediately following that meeting, our church at Pacific Union College invited some of the Glacier View delegates to give a firsthand report. The church was packed. After the initial reports from the front, there was a question-and-answer period, with roving mikes. One man toward the rear of the sanctuary jumped to his feet and asked, with gravel in his voice, "Who needs the investigative judgment, anyhow?"

Who needs the investigative judgment? *God* needs the investigative judgment—not for His information, but rather for His vindication. (God needs to be vindicated for vindicating us!) *We* need the judgment—not for our vindication, but rather for our information! The angels and the unfallen worlds need the judgment. And besides that, the prosecution—the devil and his angels—demand it. This judgment has a vital part in God's vindication before the entire universe.

As we try to understand the issues involved in the need for the pre-advent judgment, let's go back to the typical court scene of yesteryear. In those days, when they had pumps in the backyard and kerosene lamps on the oilcloth-covered tables, they often had a circuit judge who traveled from one place to another to sit in judgment on the disputes that had arisen since he was last in town. In fact, the order of events in a court trial haven't changed that much today, even in the Supreme

Court of the United States. In the first place, to have a trial there must be an accusation. Then comes the announcement that the court is going to convene. There is a hearing of the particular case involving investigation of the evidence. After the investigation, the judge or jury comes to a decision concerning the case and gives the verdict, guilty or not guilty. Finally, the sentence is pronounced and then executed.

Some time ago I had the privilege of meeting with a group of attorneys from the Lake Union Conference. At my request, these attorneys began reminiscing about the way justice was dealt in those early days of American history. Out of this discussion, a parable was born. It has the Old West flavor to it, from the time when the western frontier was Illinois. It's divided into two parts. Perhaps it will help us in understanding the purpose of the investigative judgment a bit more clearly.

The way it was

There was great excitement in the little town of Mill Creek, Illinois, that afternoon in 1845. Eighth Illinois circuit judge David Davis of Bloomingdale had just arrived. As usual, he was accompanied by several circuit lawyers, including one named Abraham Lincoln. Lincoln's presence added to the stir of excitement, for Mill Creek's citizens had not forgotten the other times when he had come to town with Judge Davis. And in addition to being an excellent lawyer, Abe Lincoln told the funniest stories anyone had ever heard.

It had been almost six months since the last court session in Mill Creek, and there was quite an accumulation of cases to be tried. Old Thomas Jacobs was suspected of setting fire to the blacksmith's shop. He and the blacksmith had had words. Old Thomas had made some pretty dark threats, and that very night the blacksmith's shop had burned to the ground. There were witnesses who said that they had seen old Thomas there at the fire, laughing like anything and slapping his knees.

Then there was the fight at the tavern between Henry Whitney and Ebenezer Bates. Whitney had finally pulled out his pistol and shot Ebenezer in cold blood. Some said that Ebenezer had asked for it and that Whitney was only defending himself. But others sided with Ebenezer and said it was murder, plain and simple.

Perhaps the most outstanding case was that of Jesse Adams. He had ridden into town one day and gone straight up to the Mill Creek Bank, shoved his gun at the teller, and demanded all the bank's cash. He'd managed to get about fifteen miles out of town before the sheriff and his deputy caught up with him. And he had been in the town jail ever since.

In addition to these more spectacular cases there were the usual disputes over property lines, debts and foreclosures, slander suits. And a man named Silas Foster had been accused of stealing pigs.

The announcement was made that court would convene the following week, and the people brought in their legal business. The lawyers went to work on the cases assigned to them. And when the time that had been announced arrived, the circuit court convened.

The whole town crowded into the courthouse, and during each recess could be heard hotly discussing the pros and cons of each case. The lawyers examined and cross-examined and called out objections at every opportunity. Abe Lincoln had a knack for bringing the truth to light, and in the cases that he defended, even the prosecuting attorney ended up admitting that he was right. As the people listened to each case and heard the evidence for themselves, they were convinced that justice was being dealt.

One by one the cases were brought before the court. The juries withdrew to deliberate, and a verdict was reached—guilty or not guilty. As Judge Davis sentenced those who had been found guilty, and acquitted those found innocent, the town was satisfied.

The last morning the judge and his lawyers were in town, there was a hanging. Henry Whitney had been found guilty of murder. And the circuit judge and his company moved on to the next town.

The second part of this parable covers the same ground. Back up and start over, please! Are you with me? This time, the story is

The way it wasn't

There was great excitement in the little town of Mill Creek, Illinois, that afternoon in 1845. Eighth Illinois circuit judge David Davis of Bloomingdale had just arrived, accompanied by Abe Lincoln and several other circuit lawyers. It has been almost six months since the last court session in Mill Creek, and there was quite an accumulation of cases to be tried.

Old Thomas Jacobs was suspected of setting fire to the blacksmith's shop. There had been a fight at the tavern between Henry Whitney and Ebenezer Bates, and Ebenezer Bates was dead. Jesse Adams was in jail awaiting trial for bank robbery. And there were the usual assortment of lesser disputes.

It was announced that court would convene immediately. The whole town crowded into the courthouse. Judge David banged his gavel on the desk and said, "Thomas Jacobs, not guilty. Silas Foster, not guilty. Henry Whitney, guilty as charged, to be hanged at sunrise. Jesse Adams, not guilty. Court is closed."

The prosecuting attorney jumped to his feet. "You can't do that," he cried. "Who do you think you are, anyway? You can't acquit these people without a fair trial or sentence them before they're proven guilty.''

The town's people sided with the prosecution. "He's right," they said. "How does the judge know who's guilty and who isn't?''

Abe Lincoln raised his voice to be heard above the tumult. "Don't you people trust the judge? The judge knows those who are his to acquit. He has been keeping tabs on things while he has been back at Bloomingdale. He has kept careful records. He has evidence, and he doesn't makes mistakes.''

But the people became even more upset. "The judge may have evidence, and he may not," they said. "But *we* don't have evidence. It's not enough just to claim to have evidence. The evidence must be examined openly before the sentence is given. The whole court needs to see the evidence, not just the judge.''

The circuit lawyers kept trying desperately to convince the people of Mill Creek that the judge could be trusted. But the people insisted that trust had to be based on an intelligent understanding of the reasons for the judge's decisions.

The last morning the judge and his lawyers were in town, there was a hanging. It was the judge who was hanged.

So much for the judge

So who needed the investigative judgment in Mill Creek? Those who were on trial needed it. The prosecution needed it. The whole town needed it. And in the end, even the judge needed it!

God was vindicated at the cross for forgiving anyone in the whole world. Through Jesus' death, sin's penalty was paid, and God can now be just and the justifier of those who believe on Him. The investigative judgment, however, shows to the universe that God is justified in forgiving the ones who *do* get forgiven. For in spite of the fact that the cross was a sufficient sacrifice

33

for the whole world, not everybody gets forgiven. And finally, the judgment during the thousand years justifies God for *not* forgiving the ones who are not forgiven. Let's go over that one more time. (1) The cross justifies God for forgiving anyone. (2) The investigative judgment justifies God for forgiving the ones who get forgiven. And (3) the thousand-year judgment justifies God for not forgiving the ones who don't get forgiven.

God is intent on getting every soul possible into His kingdom forever. But He is also intent on making sure that when He gets us there, we will be happy there forever. Could you be happy, *forever,* in heaven, if your dearest loved ones were missing and you didn't know why? God wants you to know why, and know it clearly. Because not only does He want you in heaven, and not only does He want you to be happy there, but He also is absolutely committed to handling things in such a way that the sin problem will never come again. And the investigative judgment is one of His methods of accomplishing that.

There is a group of people who are going to stand someday on a sea that looks like glass, and you, no doubt, are looking forward to being one of them. Revelation 15 says that they sing a song, called the Song of Moses and the Lamb. And in that song they sing, "Great and marvellous are thy works, Lord God Almighty; just and true are thy ways, thou King of saints." Revelation 15:3. This means that when I get to heaven, whether my loved ones are all there or not, there is a plan to enable me to still be happy forever and to still be singing from my heart, without reservation, "Just and true are thy ways, thou King of saints." So who needs the investigative judgment? You and I do.

But someone says, "Wait a minute. The investigative judgment began in 1844 and will end shortly before

Jesus comes again. We won't even be there, so how could it be for us?"

But we will be there! Do you know when you and I will attend the investigative judgment? It's when we get to heaven and have some questions, during the thousand years. Imagine stopping a passing angel and saying, "Please, is it all right to ask questions here?"

He says, "Of course. What did you want to ask?"

And you ask your question. He replies, "I'm glad you asked. We had a pre-advent judgment specifically for that purpose, and I'd like to show you what was done there." So we attend the investigative judgment during the thousand years, right? There could be no thousand years, during which time we will even judge angels, according to Scripture, if the pre-advent judgment had not taken place.

Distorted ideas about the judgment

Sometimes we have pictured the judgment as a time when the angels get out the heavenly adding machines and add up all of our good deeds and all of our bad deeds. And if we had 490 good deeds and only 480 bad deeds, we are in. I remember when I was a boy making airplanes in the sawdust while my father and uncle held their evangelistic meetings. I was thankful that my name was Venden instead of Adams—because, of course, God judges alphabetically!

We have misunderstood the purpose of the books of record that God keeps, and because of that, some have been eager to throw out the idea of books altogether. But the books are a Bible teaching. Revelation 3:5 talks about them: "He that overcometh, the same shall be clothed in white raiment; and I will not blot out his name out of the book of life, but I will confess his name before my Father, and before his angels." The books are spoken of repeatedly in Scripture. But we don't need to waste our time trying to figure out whether they have the deluxe binding or are in paperback and wondering when God will hear about computers and microfilm. The books *represent* the records that God has kept.

Can't you see God looking down at the devil's motley records, for the devil has kept a record of all the sins he has caused us to commit, and saying, "You want to keep records? All right, I'll show you how to keep records." And God keeps meticulous records, not for the purpose of keeping us out of heaven, but for the purpose of getting us into heaven in spite of the devil's charges.

There *is* a pre-advent judgment, according to Scripture. Revelation 14:6, 7 talks about it. "And I saw another angel fly in the midst of heaven, having the everlasting gospel to preach unto them that dwell on the earth, and to every nation, and kindred, and tongue, and people, saying with a loud voice, Fear God, and give glory to him; for the hour of his judgment is come: and worship him that made heaven, and earth, and the sea, and the fountains of waters." It wasn't until the time of the first angel's message that the good news could include the message that the hour of God's judgment *is* come, but it has been everlasting good news that the hour of God's judgment was coming. The fact that God has scheduled a pre-advent judgment to open the records before the entire universe, before He comes, bringing His reward with Him for every person, is good news now, and has always been.

The bad news explains the good

One of the reasons why many are having trouble accepting the good news of the judgment is that they have never really accepted the bad news of the gospel. It is the legalist who complains that the investigative-judgment teaching damages his assurance. The traditional legalist looks at the investigative judgment and begins work on becoming good enough to make it. His attention is not on Jesus and His sacrifice that is enough. It's on himself and his own works. His preoccupation betrays him as a legalist, because he is looking to works as the cause of his salvation, instead of looking to Jesus and what Jesus has already done.

The "gospel legalist" comes along and says, "It's what Jesus did at the cross that saves us." But then he betrays the fact that inside he's still on the works system of salvation when he has to get rid of the investigative judgment to *keep* his assurance! If the sacrifice of Jesus is the basis of our salvation and "Jesus paid it all, all to Him I owe," then it shouldn't disturb our assurance one iota to have our works investigated. We forget the fact that forgiveness is a gift, not something that we can earn or merit in any way. We also forget that obedience is a gift and that the only prerequisite for receiving a gift is to come into relationship with the Giver. The one who is looking to Jesus, not only for pardon, but for power in overcoming as well, can continue to look to Jesus during the time of judgment, resting in the assurance that "he which hath begun a good work in you will perform it until the day of Jesus Christ." Philippians 1:6. The fact of the judgment then becomes good news, for it means that we can look up and lift up our heads, for our redemption draweth nigh.

It is possible to do a careful study of the prophetic scriptures concerning this pillar of our faith and uncover all of the Bible support for it and still miss its significance for our own lives. (By the way, many of the apparent problems are easily solved by remembering that Daniel 7, 8, and 9 are a unit—not just Daniel 8 by itself—and should be studied together.) But our greatest need as a church is not more scholarship and research. Our greatest need is to experience the relationship and personal acquaintance with Jesus, so that we can receive His gifts of forgiveness and pardon and repentance and obedience, and yes, even the gift of assurance that comes from knowing and loving Him.

There is more involved in salvation than the onetime acceptance of Jesus' sacrifice. It's possible to have your name enrolled in the book of life, but then to have it blotted out. Matthew 24:12 says, "Because iniquity shall abound, the love of many shall wax cold. But he that shall endure unto the end, the same shall be saved." That's why the pre-advent judgment is needed. Its purpose is to *reveal*—not to discover, but to reveal—those who have not only accepted Jesus once, but who have continued to accept Him day by day, enduring to the end.

It could be bad news that those who have not become overcomers have their names blotted out of the book of life. But *I'm* not the one who overcomes—Jesus is. And if I endure to the end in the relationship with Him, He'll see to it that I'm an overcomer as well.

Freed from the devil's custody

Those who are interested in last-day events should be twice as interested in *very* last-day events. We are told that at the very end, "One interest will prevail, one subject will swallow up every other—Christ our righteousness."—*Sons and Daughters of God*, p. 259. It was predicted ninety years ago that the very last deception of Satan would be an attack on the gift of prophecy to this church—*Selected Messages*, bk. 1, p. 48. And we were told that another of the very last events would be the attempt to discredit our belief in the sanctuary doctrine.—*Counsels to Writers and Editors*, pp. 52-54. We are seeing the fulfillment of these prophecies today. But when we allow the subject of Christ our righteousness to swallow up the investigative judgment, when we see how even the judgment is part of the good news, then we are protected against

Satan's final deceptions. Truth protects!

Isn't it good news that the time is almost here when we will be freed from the devil's custody? The God of heaven has handled the great controversy in such a way that the time will come when Satan himself, by his own choice, will go to his knees and admit that God has been fair and just. "The Controversy Ended" in *The Great Controversy* tells about that dramatic moment. It's at the end of the thousand years. It's at the moment when everyone who has ever lived or died meets for the first and last time. Some are on the inside of the city, looking out; some are on the outside of the city, looking in.

The enemy is forced out of the dimension that he has been operating in, and the eyes of all turn to look on him. Isaiah 14:16, 17 says, "They that see thee shall narrowly look upon thee, and consider thee, saying, Is this the man that made the earth to tremble, that did shake kingdoms; that made the world as a wilderness, and destroyed the cities thereof; that opened not the house of his prisoners?" We'll look at him, perhaps up on a ledge somewhere, high above the throngs of people, and we'll say, "Is this the man?"

As soon as Satan has bowed and admitted that God is right, he hates himself for it. He jumps to his feet and rushes out among the millions trying to stir them for one last attempt to take the city. But his power is gone. They simply stand and stare at him. No one makes a move. Then fire comes down from heaven, and sin and sinners are no more.

Do you think that those of us within the city will be shouting and throwing our hats in the air and beating drums? No, there may be some of our loved ones out there, on the outside. And when you picture God as He sees the final end of millions of loved ones, can't you see His tears? Even Lucifer was His son, His creation, the covering cherub. And if God puts it in the hearts of fathers and mothers still to love even the wayward son or daughter, do you think God could love any less?

So in the watching crowd that day, I don't think there will be much shouting. I think we may see the Father convulsed in anguish. We may see Jesus sobbing. The angels will be weeping, and we will weep, too, as we see the Father saying Good-bye to His beloved children who refused to love Him in return.

But then the Holy Spirit, who is known as the Comforter, will bring the handkerchief and help the Father out. I'd like to be there, wouldn't you? It will be an awesome and solemn time. But because of the way God has handled the sin problem, yes, even in part because of the justice revealed through the investigative judgment, it's a scene that will never be repeated throughout all the ages of eternity.

The Bad News About the Wedding

Jesus taught the investigative judgment. If the prophecies of Daniel and Revelation look complicated, if you agree with Peter that Paul's writings are hard to understand, if your knowledge of Greek begins and ends with the single fact that *agapē* is some kind of love, then there's good news! The greatest Teacher the world has ever known taught the investigative judgment so simply that even a child can understand. The teachings of Jesus are as up-to-the-minute as today's news broadcast. And if you'd like information on any of the current issues within the church today, or tomorrow, Jesus' teachings are right to the point.

Matthew 22:1 is where we'll start for this look at one of the teachings of Jesus on the subject of the investigative judgment. "And Jesus answered and spake unto them again by parables." Notice again Jesus' favorite method of instruction—parables. In Mark 4:34 it goes so far as to say that "without a parable spake he not unto them."

Continuing with verse 2 of Matthew 22: "The kingdom of heaven is like unto a certain king, which made a marriage for his son." What does the phrase "kingdom of heaven" mean? It's another term for salvation by faith. In *The Great Controversy*, page 347, we are told, "In many of His parables Christ uses the expression 'the kingdom of heaven' to designate the work of divine grace upon the hearts of men." So one important thing to watch for in this parable is what it teaches about salvation by faith.

And the kingdom of heaven is like unto a certain king, which made a marriage for his son. If you'd like to know more about this marriage, turn to Revelation 19:9. "And he saith unto me, Write, Blessed are they which are called unto the marriage supper of the Lamb." In the context of Revelation 19 you have the time predicted when the Lamb—Jesus—gets together with His bride—the church—and the marriage takes place. It's referring to the last events just before Jesus comes again and to the time of His coming.

Now back to Matthew 22. He "sent forth his servants to call them that were bidden to the wedding: and they would not come. Again, he sent forth other servants, saying, Tell them which are bidden, Behold, I have prepared my dinner: my oxen and my fatlings are killed, and all things are ready: come unto the marriage. But they made light of it, and went their ways, one to his farm, another to his merchandise: and the remnant took his servants, and entreated them spitefully, and slew them." Verses 3-6. Here you have, in the setting of Jesus' day, the reminder to the Jewish people that their fathers had treated the prophets roughly. Being a prophet was a high-risk occupation, and the tombs of the prophets were there in reminder of that fact.

Verse 7: "But when the king heard thereof, he was wroth: and he sent forth his armies, and destroyed those murderers, and burned up their city." What was Jesus referring to here? It was a prediction of the destruction of Jerusalem, which came in A.D. 70. Verse 8: "Then saith he to his servants, The wedding is ready, but they which were bidden were not worthy. Go ye therefore into the highways, and as many as ye shall find, bid to the marriage.'' Here you have the gospel going to the Gentiles and the rest of the world in the days of the apostolic church.

Invitations for bad and good

''So those servants went out into the highways, and gathered together all as many as they found, both bad and good: and the wedding was furnished with guests.'' Verse 10. That's good news for everyone, isn't it? No one is left out. Whether you are a Pharisee or a publican, Jesus is determined to do everything possible to urge you to come to the wedding. Jesus did everything possible when He was here to reach them all—He reached Mary Magdalene and lifted her above her life of sin. He reached Simon the Pharisee and showed him his need of salvation. He loved Pharisees and Sadducees and harlots and thieves and the laboring class. He sent out the invitation to all, both bad and good, and that should include every one of us today as well. The wedding was furnished with guests.

But now the plot thickens. In the days of Christ, it was customary for a wealthy person, a king in particular, when he put on a wedding for his son, to send not only an invitation, but also to send a wedding garment for the person to wear. That solved a lot of problems. Can you imagine receiving an invitation to the wedding of a king's son? What would be the first thing the wife would say? ''What am I going to wear?'' For them, that problem was already solved. So it made no difference whether you were rich or poor, whether you were in the palace or in the gutter. Even the poorest who received an invitation to the wedding of the king's son could go dressed like a millionaire.

The king went to a great deal of expense to provide the wedding garments. If anyone were to show up at the wedding without the wedding garment on, it would be an insult to the king, it would be an insult to the king's son, and, in a sense, the whole kingdom would feel the sting.

With that in mind, let's go on to verse 11. "And when the king came in to see the guests, he saw there a man which had not on a wedding garment." Evidently the king comes in to see the guests *before* the wedding supper of the king's son takes place. The king comes in to see the guests—to examine the guests—could we go so far as to say he "investigated" the guests? "And when the king came in to see the guests, he saw there a man which had not on a wedding garment." Well, you say, he probably had on his Sabbath suit. Or perhaps a jogging outfit. Or sweatshirt and Levis. No, he was naked. Turn to Revelation 3:17. The people who lacked the righteousness of Christ are wretched and miserable and poor and blind and what? Naked. So this man had the audacity to show up at the wedding naked.

The very most you could manage, scripturally, would be for him to have on some filthy rags, for all of our righteousnesses are as filthy rags. Isaiah 64:6. But notice how the king treated him. Verse 12. "And he saith unto him, Friend." Isn't that good news? He said, "Friend, how camest thou in hither not having a wedding garment?" Was there some misunderstanding? You must have received the invitation, because you are here. But what about the wedding garment? Didn't the package arrive? Do you have an explanation? Would you like to say something? He treated him with dignity.

He was speechless

But the Bible says the man was speechless. The reason people are speechless is usually because they have nothing to say. And it was only then that the king said to the servants, "Bind him hand and foot, and take him away, and cast him into outer darkness; there shall be weeping and gnashing of teeth." Verse 13. And the king must have been weeping too. "For many are called, but few are chosen." Verse 14.

We have all been invited to the marriage supper of the Lamb. The friendly arms of the cross still point the way to the heavenly country, and Jesus did pay it all. When Jesus bowed His head and died, He purchased the right to forgive anyone who was ever born into this world who would accept His forgiveness. The invitation is out today to the marriage supper of the Lamb.

The invitation, and our acceptance of that invitation, is what is involved in justification by faith. "For by grace are ye saved through faith; and that not of yourselves: it is the gift of God: not of works, lest any man should boast." Ephesians 2:8, 9.

The invitation to the wedding and the acceptance of that invitation is not the only part of the story, however. There's the wedding garment as well. It's not enough that the king wears a wedding garment. It's not even enough that the king's son has on a wedding garment. Each and every guest must wear a wedding garment, or he will find himself in outer darkness instead of at the marriage supper. And that would be bad news! The examination, the investigation by the king, includes more than checking to see who has responded to the invitation. He is looking for those who are wearing the wedding garment as well.

Let's go back to Revelation 19:6-8 to find out what the wedding garment is. "And I heard as it were the voice of a great multitude, and as the voice of many waters, and as the voice of mighty thunderings, saying, Alleluia: for the Lord God omnipotent reigneth. Let us be glad and rejoice, and give honour to him: for the marriage of the Lamb is come, and his wife hath made herself ready. And to her was granted that she should be arrayed in fine linen, clean and white: for the fine linen is the righteousness of the saints.'' And some of the other versions say, accurately, "The linen is the good *deeds* of God's people" (TEV), "Fine linen stands for the righteous *acts* of the saints" (NIV), "For the fine linen is the righteous deeds of the saints" (RSV).

But wait a minute. Can anyone, saints or otherwise, produce righteousness? Can saints produce good deeds? Jeremiah 23:6 says that the Lord is our righteousness. So any kind of good deeds or righteousness that you see in the saints is the Lord at work. But notice that this righteousness in Revelation 19 is not His righteousness in my place. It's not a substitute righteousness; it is His righteousness lived out in the life. So this wedding garment represents the second phase of salvation by faith alone, the area of sanctification, of living the Christian life, of the work that God wants to do *in* us.

For the honor of the king

So when the king came in to examine the guests, he saw there a man who hadn't put on the wedding garment. Evidently the man wanted the invitation, he wanted to be at the wedding, but he still had refused to put on the wedding garment.

"Of those who accepted the invitation, there were some who thought only of benefiting themselves. They came to share the provisions of the feast, but had no desire to honor the king."—*Christ's Object Lessons,* p. 309. Let's paraphrase that. There are some who are interested in getting themselves to heaven, but they have no desire to accept Christ's righteousness in their lives, to bring honor to Him. "Let your light so shine before men, that they may see your good works, and glorify your Father which is in heaven." Matthew 5:16. He leads me in the paths of righteousness for whose name's sake? For *His* name's sake.

If your primary purpose for being a Christian is to get yourself to heaven, you may never arrive. Of course, we should be interested in getting to heaven. But once we have accepted Jesus, our getting to heaven is certain. Now there's bigger business—to bring honor and glory to the King and His Son.

"By the wedding garment in the parable is represented the pure, spotless character which Christ's true followers will possess." "This robe, woven in the loom of heaven, has in it not one thread of human devising."—*Christ's Object Lessons*, pp. 310, 311. Please notice that sanctification—Christ living His life out in me through the Holy Spirit—obedience, victory, and overcoming have in them not one thread of human devising. All we can do is accept them as gifts. "By His perfect obedience He has made it possible for every human being to obey God's commandments. When we submit ourselves to Christ, the heart is united with His heart, the will is merged in His will, the mind becomes one with His mind, the thoughts are brought into captivity to Him; we live His life. This is what it means to be clothed with the garment of His righteousness."—*Ibid.*, p. 312.

The power to live as Jesus lived, in dependence upon God, is available to us today. It is possible for us to put on the wedding garment, to accept of Christ's righteousness in our lives, and thus bring honor and glory to the King of heaven.

Once saved always saved as long as you keep saved

Some years ago I was in love with a beautiful girl. She lived in San Francisco, and I lived in Los Angeles. The day came that we had agreed to become husband and wife. I drove to San Francisco, where her parents were putting on the wedding. As we stood before the preacher he said, "Do you?" And I said, "Yes." And he asked her, "Do you?" And she said, "Yes." And he said, "You are."

After the wedding, she went home with her folks, and I went back to Los Angeles. Two years later someone said, "Are you married?"

And I said, "Yes."

They said, "We never see your wife."

And I replied, "I haven't seen her either, for two years."

"Do you write to her?"

"No."

"Do you telephone?"

"No."

"And you're *married?*"

I said, "Yes, I said 'I do.' I have a certificate to prove it."

And they said, "You'd better check on that!"

This *is* a parable, by the way! But if someone were to have investigated my marriage under such conditions, they might find that the marriage was no more. There are people who have joined the church twenty years ago, who have accepted Jesus, but who have done nothing about it since. An investigation could very well reveal that their salvation was to be seriously questioned. We believe in once married, always married, *as long as you keep married.* And we believe in once saved, always saved, *as long as you keep saved.*

Marriage is based on a relationship. When there is no more relationship, there is no more marriage. Salvation is also based on a relationship, and without that relationship, and communication, the salvation is no longer present. John 17:3; Matthew 7:23. You are a Christian today if you have a present-tense relationship with Jesus. And for those who endure unto the end in their relationship with Christ, it is certain that they will be overcomers as well. So when the King

48

comes in to examine the guests, He is coming to reveal who has endured to the end and who has become an overcomer.

But I'm not an overcomer yet

"Well," you say, "I'm not doing very well on that. I haven't yet become an overcomer. I still fall and fail." I'd like to remind you that overcoming is God's department; it's not yours. Obedience is God's department. It comes by faith alone in Jesus Christ. It isn't something we achieve; it's something we receive. Victory isn't something that we strive for, try for, or work hard to get. It's something that comes as a by-product of the faith relationship. Putting on the wedding garment is simply accepting the gift that God has given, sanctification, in the same way that we receive the gift of justification. And even the Christian world of today is still waiting to hear that good news. It's part of our special message as the remnant people.

Yet most of us continue to work hard, trying to be overcomers. That's the reason we don't overcome—because you can't work for a gift. To try to earn a gift is an insult to the giver. The wedding garment is free. The King Himself has provided it for us. All we need to do is to accept it.

Jesus said, speaking of the Holy Spirit which is the avenue by which we accept His gift of overcoming, "If any man thirst, let him come unto me, and drink. He that believeth on me, as the scriptures hath said, out of his belly shall flow rivers of living water." John 7:37, 38.

Are you thirsty for the water of life? Perhaps you will be able to identify with the man in this parable.

If any man thirst

Ed didn't feel very well. His mouth was terribly dry. His throat ached. His skin was hot. And his lips were

49

beginning to crack. He didn't seem to have much energy either. Even the slightest exertion made him feel light-headed and dizzy, and several times a day he would become so faint and weak that he would fall. Whenever that happened, he really got discouraged.

One day, as Ed lay huddled at the bottom of the porch steps where he had just fallen, he made a decision. "Surely I don't have to be like this for the rest of my life. I'm going to try to get some help."

So he went to visit Dr. Smith. Dr. Smith listened carefully to all of his symptoms and then nodded his head. "Ed, your problem is that you are thirsty. It's a common enough ailment. In fact, in recent years it has seemed that there are more and more thirsty people seeking help than ever before."

Ed felt relieved. "Thanks, doctor," he said. "What shall I do about it?"

Dr. Smith leaned back in his chair. "Well, first of all, try to decide what it is that bothers you the most. Is it the dry mouth, the cracked lips, or what? Let's say, for example, that your cracked lips bother you more than anything. Then go to work on those cracked lips. Give 'em all you've got. After they're healed up, then maybe start to work on your dizzy spells. Don't try to do everything at once. Overcoming these symptoms is a lifetime process. Use your willpower. Make your choice to work on these things, and stick with it."

"Thanks, Dr. Smith," said Ed. But after he got back home he puzzled. "I should have asked more exactly how to do it," he thought. After several days of repeating over and over, 'I choose not to get dizzy, I choose not to get dizzy," he was dizzier than ever. So he went back to the office. "Dr. Smith, I've tried, but maybe there's something I didn't understand. I'm still as thirsty as ever," Ed said sadly.

"Have you really tried? You've got to give it all you've got, you know," Dr. Smith said sternly.

50

"Well, maybe I haven't tried as hard as I might have," Ed admitted. "But isn't there something more tangible that I could do?"

Dr. Smith smiled. "Yes, I guess there is. Science has been discovering a very close connection between health and exercise. Why don't you try doing 200 push-ups a day?"

Ed went home again, but after only seven push-ups he collapsed and had to spend the rest of the day in bed. The next morning he called Dr. Smith.

"If you won't do what I tell you, why waste your time and mine by coming back?" Dr. Smith demanded.

"But, doctor, isn't there anything else?" Ed insisted.

"Well," Dr. Smith answered reluctantly, "for some extreme cases a health spa is the answer. If you won't do the exercises by yourself, perhaps the stimulation of a group would help you."

So Ed paid a hundred dollars to join the spa, but after the first session, when he fainted from doing only four push-ups, he was too ashamed to return. Still, his thirst was no better. So he tried another doctor.

When you're thirsty, you need water!

Dr. Jones heard Ed's story and said cheerfully, "Why Ed, how unfortunate Dr. Smith didn't explain to you. I'm sure he knows. What you need when you are thirsty is water."

"Water?" Ed asked, hope beginning to flicker in his eyes. "That does sound appealing. Where can I find water?"

"It comes from a well. So I would recommend that you get a shovel and dig yourself a well."

Ed went home joyfully. He got a good shovel and started to dig, but after digging for only five minutes he passed out. When he came to, his next-door neighbor was bending over him. "Ed, whatever are you doing?"

"I'm digging a well. I need water," he said.

"Why haven't you heard? There's a well already dug. All you have to do is go and get it. The Owner of the well will give you, for free, all the water you need. In fact, He guarantees that if you'll come and drink from His well, every day, you'll never be thirsty again."

"Really?"

"Yes, why don't you try it."

"Well," said Ed, "I'd better check with my doctor first."

So he stumbled back to Dr. Jones and told him the news. Dr. Jones shook his head. "I've heard of it, Ed. But I don't recommend it. I think myself that if you'll dig your own well, you'll appreciate the water so much more than if it's just handed to you. Better keep digging. God helps those who help themselves."

Ed went back to his digging, but it soon became apparent that he was going to die before he could dig deep enough. Why, after several days he had only dug a hole three inches deep. And he was failing fast.

So in complete helplessness, he gave up on digging his own well and went to the Owner of the well and said, "Unless You give me water, I'll die."

The Owner of the well said gently, "Everyone who comes to My well can have all the water he wants to satisfy his thirst. You never need thirst again."

Ed accepted the first free gift of water from the well, and immediately something began to happen inside of him. His mouth wasn't so dry anymore. His throat was soothed. Day by day, as he returned to the well to drink, his symptoms began to disappear.

Now he's jogging around the countryside telling everyone he meets the good news—that the water is free.

Good News for Legalists

I have a friend who is a Bible worker in the Pacific Union. She is a senior citizen now. Her name is Mary Walch. She's still getting people out of bed in the morning and out of bed at night to study the Bible. And whenever she hears anyone downing legalism, she gets upset. She says, "I *am* a legalist. I'm glad to be a legalist."

Her definition of legalism, however, is that a legalist is one who believes in the law of God. In that case, then, every Seventh-day Adventist ought to be a legalist. Every Christian ought to be a legalist.

But the usual definition of a legalist is a little different color from that, isn't it? The usual definition of a legalist is one who is trying to work his way to heaven by keeping the law. A legalist is one who depends on his good deeds to earn his salvation. A legalist is one who thinks that being good is what makes a person a Christian. And if there's anything that the apostle Paul is against in his writings, it's the idea that the law can ever be used as a method of salvation.

However, I would like to go a step further and give you an additional definition of a legalist. A legalist is anyone who has hope of salvation who is living life apart from Jesus. Anyone who hopes to be saved, but who is living at a distance from the Lord Jesus, has no other choice—he's depending on his own works to get him to heaven. That's the only other option. So if the surveys are correct, and if three quarters of the members of our church have no time for God or the Bible or prayer or personal devotions day by day, then three quarters of the church members are legalists.

You and I were born legalists. Everyone in this world has suffered from the disease of legalism to one degree or another. Every day we experience it, and even though we might have a theory of faith alone in Jesus Christ, it's only the daily acceptance of the grace of God that can in practice keep us above the life of the legalist.

This can get a little tricky, because there are two different kinds of legalists. There is the black legalist and the scarlet legalist! We might call them the rigid legalists and the liberal legalists. By the black legalist, I mean the one who has the black suit, black tie, black shoes, black socks, and a long face! He finds his security in the standards of the church that he upholds, and he judges everyone else who falls short of his achievements. (From his viewpoint, practically everyone else *does* fall short, by the way!) He's the Pharisee, and his outward performance is well controlled.

The scarlet legalist is described in Revelation—the woman who is clothed in scarlet and adorned with jewels, etc. This type of legalist is reacting against the old-guard form of legalism. This person wears jewelry and makeup, goes to the movies, is not particular in regard to Sabbath observance, and takes real pride in the fact that she is no longer legalistic. But both kinds of legalists are deceived. They are as legalistic as ever, but just afflicted with different forms of the same disease. The liberal legalist is as much a legalist as the rigid one, for both know nothing of the personal relationship with Jesus. Both of them are trusting to their own ways instead of trusting in Christ, who alone has the power to give salvation.

Good news and bad news

Let's read the good news and bad news for legalists, beginning with verse 30 of Romans 9. "What shall we say then? That the Gentiles, which followed not after righteousness, have attained to righteousness, even the righteousness which is of faith. But Israel, which followed after the law of righteousness, hath not attained to the law of righteousness. Wherefore? [Why?] Because they sought it not by faith, but as it were by the works of the law."

This was the problem of the religious world back then—people trying to save themselves by their own works in keeping the law. And it says, "For they stumbled at that stumblingstone; as it is written, Behold, I lay in Sion a stumblingstone and rock of offence: and whosoever believeth on him shall not be ashamed." Verses 32, 33. Who is the stumbling stone? Jesus.

Continuing with chapter 10, verses 1-4. "Brethren, my heart's desire and prayer to God for Israel is, that they might be saved. For I bear them record that they have a zeal of God, but not according to knowledge. For they being ignorant of God's righteousness, and going about to establish their own righteousness, have not submitted [surrendered] them*selves* unto the righteousness of God. For Christ is the end of the law for righteousness to every one that believeth." (Emphasis added.) Please notice that the verse doesn't say Christ is the end of the law, but that Christ is the end of the law *for righteousness* to every one that believeth.

There is bad news for legalists in this passage, because they will never attain to righteousness by working on it, no matter how hard they work. But there is also good news for legalists, because they don't have to keep wearing themselves out with fruitless effort. Christ is the end of the law for righteousness for everyone that believeth. And that's good news, especially for legalists!

It's the legalist who has been working the hardest on trying to gain salvation. And the words of Christ's friendly invitation, "Come unto me, all ye that labour and are heavy laden, and I will give you rest" (Matthew 11:28), can be the best news the legalist has ever heard, when their meaning finally comes clear. It is good news to hear and accept that Christ is the end of the law for righteousness to every one that believeth.

How to be an overcomer without becoming a legalist

In spite of the fact that we can never attain to righteousness by our good deeds and our obedience, the fact remains that the subject of obedience and victory is still important in the Christian life. Even the legalist recognizes that the subject of overcoming must be handled somehow. The scarlet legalist concludes that victory is not needed, maybe not even possible. But this theory doesn't even hold up to logic and reason, much less to Scripture. For even the most liberal legalist, who has lowered the standard in place of improving performance, will agree that there *are* limits. Let's say you're having problems with church standards, and you scrap the church standards. That may appear to work out—if it's attending movies that you're having problems with. But what if your problem is that you are a murderer or a child abuser or you can't stop robbing banks? How low can the standard go? The liberal legalist is able to meet the liberal standard today, but what about the more liberal legalist who would like to see a more liberal standard? Suppose you were to find that you couldn't even join the liberal legalists, because your willpower was so weak that you couldn't even force yourself to meet the lowest standard of performance? What then?

On the other hand, for too long the rigid, traditional legalist has met all evidence of weakness on the part of others as simply an evidence of lack of sincerity. They look scornfully at the struggling sinner and say, "If you really wanted to, you could overcome. If you would *really* try, you'd make it." And the one who has failed has not only the guilt of defeat but the additional burden of being considered insincere and hypocritical as well.

There has to be good news for both types of legalists. There has to be a third option. And there is! It's the option of relationship with Christ. To all of the legalists of His day—to the liberals who wanted the standard lowered, as well as to the traditionalists who wanted the standard even more rigid—Jesus came and offered Himself. Christ was the end of the law for righteousness then. And He is the end of the law for righteousness today, for those of us who trust in Him.

But being the born legalists that we all are, we find it hard to understand how this works. We accept the theory that works is not where it's at. We admit that it's good news. And then we try to figure out how it actually works in practical life. I received a letter that expressed the dilemma very well. I have carried it around in my files for several years now. The paper is faded, but its content is still fresh. It was written by a young minister's wife, a brilliant woman who had studied the Greek and Hebrew and who was a theologian in her own right. But she was still trying to grasp the practical side of the good news for legalists. It was written on blue paper, so I have come to call it the "blue letter."

The blue letter

"Help! I have some questions I thought were answered a couple of years ago, so elementary I hesitate

57

to ask them. Please overlook the baby Christian ideas and tell me what you have discovered, since you have been on the route longer than I have. This business of the will: How far do we take it? In giving our will to God, is that all we have to do?

"To clarify, here's an example. And that's all it is, it is not the problem—just an example. But the principles might apply. How does one go about fighting his appetite? Does he just tell God he can't control it, ask Him to control it for him, and give Him his will? And then let God make him not want to eat?

"In the meantime, when he's hungry, should he take diet pills to help God out? Stay busy all day to keep from food? Run out of the kitchen so he won't be tempted? Or just say, 'OK, God. You do whatever You want with my will, including controlling my appetite. I can't. So the rest is up to You.' Do you claim the promises that God will and do in you, according to His good pleasure, and then sit back and eat while you are waiting for God to change your will and actions?

"When God gets me to the place where I don't want to eat because I know it is against God's will [right here the illustration breaks down—last I heard, God was in favor of eating!] and I don't want to hurt Him, but I still want to eat because it tastes good, should I go ahead and eat while I wait for God to take away the desire? Or should I exercise my willpower and try not to? What is this relationship between will and willpower? When I ask God to wash away my sins and give me a new heart, am I to believe He does this because He has promised? Then do I just wait for Him to do it all, no matter how long it takes—the don't-sweat-it-just-surrender philosophy? Does God take away the food or the appetite? Will He answer prayer for other things while the appetite indulgence continues?

"I have read a lot of answers and promises, in the Bible and spirit of prophecy and other places, I've experienced the solution to many problems—but this time I'm baffled. Maybe I'm impatient or looking for an easy way out. But I think I am being honest with God and myself. How literal are these instructions? I am anxious for your reply because the hang-up hangs on!"

How would you answer?

Soon after I received the "blue letter," I took it with me to a minister's meeting and began to ask around for some answers from my colleagues. One person said, "She doesn't have enough faith." Another said, "She's impatient. She should give God more time." Someone else said, "I think she really has a problem!" And I said, "Thanks a lot!"

Someone said, "God will sometimes give us a thorn in the flesh to keep us humble." Someone said, "No one's perfect." Someone said, "Maybe she has a hormone problem!" Someone said, "I'd need more detail before I could give an answer." On and on the answers came. The question of obedience and overcoming and victory is by no means that clear in our minds. And the nearer we come to the closing scenes, to the time of the judgment, the more anxious we become.

There are people everywhere who know about the eschatology, and they can't miss the evidence that things are just about over. And they say, "If I'm supposed to be perfect and be one of these overcomers by such and such a time, then I'm going to have to do better than I'm doing now." And this is precisely why some have made a major shift in their theology in recent times. They know, according to their present and past performance, that they aren't going to make it. So they shift their theology to meet their experience.

In so doing, perhaps they are missing one of the greatest avenues that God has in mind to enable them to be overcomers—that of coming to the end of their own resources. It is because we thought we were doing pretty well and because we figured we had plenty of time and because we have thought we could become overcomers if we tried a little harder and a little longer that we have waited so long to surrender, to submit ourselves to God, to give up on the hope that we could ever succeed in our own strength. "They that be whole need not a physician, but they that are sick." Matthew 9:12. Is it possible that one of the major reasons why we are not yet whole is that we have not yet admitted to being sick and so have not come to the Great Physician for healing?

I knew a woman one time who was ready to become a Seventh-day Adventist except for one thing: She couldn't stop smoking. She couldn't understand her own problem. She had experienced a marvelous deliverance from alcohol and from some of her other problems. But her problem with smoking persisted. After my family and I had moved on to another town, one day I received a phone call from this woman. She was dying of lung cancer and was calling from the hospital where she was awaiting surgery. She asked me to pray with her. And then she said, "By the way, I've quit smoking."

I said, "How did that happen?"

And she replied, "I had to!"

As I questioned her further, she told me two things. First, she had never thought that smoking was that big a deal. She could see giving up the drinking. She could see the adverse effect it had on her behavior when she was drunk. But smoking? No biggie. What was so bad about smoking? And, second, she had always thought that she could stop smoking any time she wanted to. Sure, the drinking had been something she couldn't control. She had been compelled to give up on that and allow God to *give* her the victory. But when it came to smoking, she had thought she could handle that herself. She thought will power was enough.

When the smoke began to rise for her personally, when she developed the lung cancer, she was brought face-to-face with two facts. One, smoking *was* a biggie. It was deadly. And two, she had found that she was as helpless to control her desire for cigarettes as she had been to control her desire for alcohol. But she had continued her relationship with the Lord Jesus, and once she recognized and admitted the desperate situation she was in and her need of God's power, she was enabled to receive the gift of victory over her smoking as well.

Surrender means giving up

No one ever surrendered to the other side while he still thought he could win the war. Surrender comes only after all hope of winning is gone. The reason why we have not surrendered in the first place, or not stayed surrendered in the second place, is that our legalistic natures keep rising to the top, and we keep hoping that perhaps if we fight a little harder or a little longer, we can win by ourselves.

Have you ever come to the end of your rope on a particular problem, turned it over to God, and experienced victory that comes as a gift from Him? And then have you ever stayed in that position for a period of time, only to have the devil come and tempt you this way? "You're doing great on overcoming that sin. Now that you've broken the habit of sinning and are in practice with the overcoming bit, you can handle it yourself." And as soon as you try, you fall again. Have you seen it happen? And so we fluctuate back and forth between surrender to God and trying to manage things on our own.

What will finally happen is that we will run out of time. For those who are absolutely locked in on the relationship with Christ but who have run out of time in learning how to be overcomers, there is only one alternative left. It's the alternative God has been trying to bring us to all along—it's to give up. Completely. Forever. And when we finally realize the deadly results of the sin problem we have been trying to handle on our own and at the same time how helpless we are to handle sin on our own, we will give up on even attempting to overcome in our own strength. And once we have given up—finally, completely, totally—we will learn what Paul learned when he said, "When I am weak, then am I strong." 2 Corinthians 12:10.

The bottom line

In all of the discussion and dialogue and debate in our church today, there is one common thread. It is often disguised, but the basic issue is whether obedience comes by faith alone in Jesus Christ or by our own hard work. Let me explain why this is the bottom line. If my obedience is something that I work on myself, then my end product will be filthy rags. Even if I go so far as to say, "Well, God is going to have to *help* me," as long as I rely on myself to do any part of it, my end product is going to be, to any extent I am involved, filthy rags. Any kind of righteousness or obedience or victory or overcoming that I am in any way trying to produce is going to be imperfect. I have no other option, right? If that's true, then it would be impossible for me to keep God's commandments.

But the remnant people spoken of in Revelation are those who *do* keep God's commandments. It is the overcomers whose names are retained in the book of life during the time of the judgment. So there must be a way of obeying God and keeping His commandments that has escaped some of us. We need to understnd something. What is it? It is that obedience comes by faith alone in Jesus Christ. This means that we must come into a relationship of absolute dependence upon

Him. This relationship allows Him to do what He has always wanted to do—*live His life in us*. Then He wills and does according to His good pleasure. And whatever Jesus does is real obedience through and through. So the person who believes that obedience comes through faith alone, through dependence upon Jesus who brings the power, also believes that it is possible for Jesus to obey God's commandments within the depending person.

For a long time the church has held two incompatible beliefs. One is that we can keep God's commandments, that we can overcome. Some have even dealt with things like perfection. The other is that while we do need God's help, we are supposed to work hard on our own obedience. Those two are incompatible.

At least the "new theology" emphasis is consistent in that area. They say, Yes, you *are* supposed to work hard on your own obedience and do the best you can. But you cannot obey, you cannot overcome, you cannot keep God's commandments. At least they are consistent, for the two go together.

The time will come when we will have to either join the "new theology" and reject the possibility of overcoming, or we will have to find out what obedience by faith alone in Jesus Christ is all about.

Obedience by faith alone

Obedience can come by faith alone—the Bible says so! Romans 1:17: "The just shall *live* by faith." The just are those who have accepted justification by faith. Those *are* the just. Living the Christian life is understood to be part of sanctification. So Paul is saying that those who have been justified by faith are to be sanctified by faith as well. This in no way does away with works. To the contrary, only the one who lives by faith alone is able to do the works. "The just shall *live* by faith."

In John 15:5 Jesus says,"Without me ye can do nothing." But Philippians 4:13 says, "I can do all things through Christ." So the conclusion is that we must get with Him, through communication, through relationship, through time spent with Jesus day by day. And that's the very thing that three fourths of the church is not doing. This lack of relationship is the reason we get panicky when we see that the end is right upon us. We have forgotten that the entire basis of the Christian life is the fellowship and relationship with Jesus day by day. We spend our time and effort trying to be good. But we forget that the Christian is one who knows Jesus personally.

The only alternative to legalism today is relationship with Jesus. It's good news to the one who has been working on his behavior, trying to do his duty, trying to do what's right, trying to learn that there is a much higher motivation available. That motivation is the power of love. As we learn to know Jesus, we will learn to love Him. Love for Him will change our desires, our motives, our hearts. The obedience that seemed to be either an unpleasant duty or a total impossibility now becomes the most natural thing in the world. For we become changed into His image—by beholding Him. Duty becomes a delight and sacrifice a pleasure. And the news that Jesus' coming is right upon us becomes good news—terrific news—even for legalists!

Good News for Pharisees

Have you ever played the game called follow-the-leader? Boys and girls have played it for years. I can remember leading the other kids in the neighborhood through the swimming pool with their clothes on, through the mud, and off the highest steps on the porch, and any other ridiculous place I could think of. They came right along behind, because we were playing follow-the-leader. And even though follow-the-leader is considered a childhood game, most of us continue to play it one way or another. The entire advertising industry is built on this tendency of human beings to follow the leader, to do what they see someone else, some leader, doing.

Sheep are notorious for following the leader. At a slaughterhouse in New York City, a goat was trained to jump into the chute as soon as the gate opened. The sheep followed. Just before the slaughtering section, there was a little side door. When the goat reached that point he jumped out, the side door slammed shut behind him, and the sheep kept going. The goat went back for another group. The people at the slaughterhouse had come up with an appropriate name for the goat—Judas! And the game of follow-the-leader ended up tragically, at least for the sheep.

5-G.N.B.N.

Following religious leaders

At the time of Christ, people followed religious leaders. There were two main groups, the Pharisees and the Sadducees. The leaders were off course, and the people followed. Both leaders and people went astray. Jesus told a parable about this follow-the-leader syndrome, perhaps one of the shortest parables He ever told. It's found in Luke 6:39, 40. "And he spake a parable unto them, Can the blind lead the blind? shall they not both fall into the ditch? The disciple is not above his master: but every one that is perfect shall be as his master." The NIV says, "A student is not above his teacher, but everyone who is fully trained will be like his teacher." Perhaps we could paraphrase it this way, "The followers will invariably be like their leaders, and rarely will a follower rise above his leader."

We could mention one name—Hitler—to give a classic example of the danger of people following blindly the leading of other people. And the German people are no more gullible than the rest of us. All of us are prone to follow leaders. Sometimes the most self-centered leader is the one who attracts the most self-centered followers. The tragedy in the days of Christ was that a whole nation perished because they went blindly following their religious leaders instead of studying Scripture for themselves. The great danger we face as a church today is that we will depend upon other people. This is one of the primary reasons for disunity. We are not in the habit of studying Scripture for ourselves. Many study a lot of the teachings of various leaders, but not so many study the *Scripture* for themselves.

One of the hazards of talking about leaders is that some people immediately think of Washington, D.C. I'd like to assure you that this is not an attack on the official church leadership. People often choose for leaders those who have no official leading position in the organized church structure. This is rather a warning against following *anyone*, regardless of his occupation. We are to be followers of Christ. No leader is to be followed blindly, even though most people who do so wouldn't admit to blindness. The proper function of a leader is to help people to see for themselves.

We need leaders. God believes in leadership. According to Scripture even heaven has its system of leadership. But the function of the leader is to lead the people to know Jesus for themselves. The purpose of leadership is not to hand truth to people for them to accept without any further investigation. There's an old adage which says, "You can give a man a fish, and you will feed him for a day. You can teach a man to fish, and you will feed him for a lifetime." And while that isn't a very vegetarian illustration, it still speaks the truth. Paul was a mighty leader in the early church. He was not blind, and he taught the truth he received from God. But the Bereans checked it out for themselves. They had the perfect combination. Their lesson to us is this: if we are in the habit of checking truth for ourselves, we will not be misled.

Who were the Pharisees and Sadducees?

The Pharisees and Sadducees at the time of Christ were only representatives of the entire nation. The people who followed the Sadducees became like their leaders. The people who followed the Pharisees became pharisaical. We're not just having a history lesson when we look at these religious leaders from the time of Christ, because their characteristics are still present in the church today, both in leaders and followers, for those on every level of the church who are spiritually blind.

In terms of behavior the Pharisees were the conservatives and the Sadducees were the liberals.

The Pharisees observed many more rites and ceremonies and traditions than did the Sadducees. But both groups were legalists because both had their attention on their performance instead of upon God.

The Pharisees were traditionalists, according to Mark 7 and Matthew 15, and were very loyal in their support of that which had been handed down from the fathers. The Sadducees were the intellectuals who loved to discuss hard questions, such as the marriage state in heaven. The Pharisees were perfectionists. The Sadducees were imperfectionists.

The Sadducees didn't believe in resurrection from the dead, physically or spiritually. They did not believe in the power of God worked out in the life. They did not accept the judgment and believed that only the first five books of the Scripture were inspired. Among the Sadducees were some of Jesus' worst enemies.

The Pharisees and Sadducees were violently opposed to each other. The Jewish nation at the time of Christ had much theological discord. The people lined up behind the leaders, some following Pharisees, some following Sadducees.

Neither group, Pharisees or Sadducees, was converted to Christ. Neither group could offer a realistic hope of salvation to the weak person. Neither group had time for the harlots and thieves and publicans. Both groups misinterpreted Scripture, misinterpreted the law, misinterpreted prophecy, and misinterpreted the kingdom of heaven that Jesus taught. The principle that man can save himself by his own righteousness was the principle of both groups, even though they had a great *theory* of justification and the blood of the lambs flowed freely at their sacrificial services.

Jesus called both groups hypocrites because of their external religion. The essence of Christ's teaching, which was self-surrender, found no acceptance in their thinking or experience. Neither group had experienced the supernatural work of the Spirit upon the heart. They had never experienced the new capacity for knowing God, which is not even present in the unconverted heart. That's why there was so little meaningful Scripture study, so little truly private prayer, so little relationship with God. The capacity wasn't even there. And while these hypocrites were meticulous Sabbath keepers and tithe payers and health reformers, there was so little on the inside that responded to the truths of God's Word, that they ended up tying the Scriptures to their wrists and foreheads in an attempt to substitute for what they lacked on the inside. There was no room for God's Word in their hearts. Self was the center of their focus. Nobody is more selfish than a Pharisee. And the new birth, which would have brought about the death of the Pharisee, because it changes the heart, was threatening to those who were interested only in changing the outside.

Pharisees and Sadducees don't like Jesus

The religious leaders didn't like Jesus because He received sinners—the open sinners whom they despised. They didn't like Jesus because He was more interested in the true meaning of the Sabbath than in the external regulations they had invented. They didn't like Jesus because He didn't observe their traditions, fasts, washings, and ceremonies. They didn't like Jesus because He wasn't impressed with their external goodness. They didn't like Jesus because of His teaching of self-surrender, the very thing they feared more than anything else. They didn't like Jesus because He didn't live up to their expectations as a Messiah. They didn't like Jesus because He did not treat them with the respect they craved. And most of all, they didn't like Jesus because of the condemnation they felt in His presence. The Pharisees and Sadducees were victims of salvation by works, and in spite of the meticulous appearance they tried to maintain before the crowds, they all had their problems behind the barn. This made them uneasy in the presence of Jesus, whose purity was a rebuke to their sins. They didn't like Jesus, because they didn't want to give up on the idea of saving themselves.

Another reason why they didn't like Jesus was the manner of His coming. They had expected that the religious leaders would be the first to herald the coming of the Messiah. To be passed by, to be informed of His birth by ignorant shepherds and heathens from another country, was more than their pride could take. They refused to accept that God could be trying to communicate to them through these channels. Once they had made their position public, they were too proud to retract it and continued to the end to deny the testimony of their own senses.

Their motivation for being religious was an attempt to gain the temporal blessings that came as a result of moral living. They liked to see the grasshoppers stopped at the line fence when they had paid their tithe. They liked the respect of the people. And although they were at swords' points with one another, they finally united in the end at the crucifixion of Jesus. Both groups were legalists, both groups were against Jesus, and both groups were wrong.

It's true that they had a limited acceptance of Jesus—let's face it. They didn't reject Him altogether, in spite of the fact that they didn't like Him. They believed Him to be a prophet. They accepted Him as a miracle-worker and healer. They accepted Him as a great teacher. But they did not accept Jesus as Saviour, Lord, and God. Lordship is where they drew the line. And their limited acceptance led to total rejection in the end. The people, who were following blindly along, also ended up rejecting Jesus, in spite of the tremendous evidence that He was exactly who He claimed to be. The people were sometimes astonished at the lack of acceptance Jesus found with their leaders, but they continued in the end to follow the leaders they had chosen.

Could it be possible to be in the camp of the Pharisee or Sadducee today? Is it still possible to be a conservative legalist, who hopes to get into heaven by his own works? Is it possible to be a great defender of the traditions that have been handed down from the fathers and still to miss recognizing and accepting the living Christ? Or is it possible to be a Sadducee today, who finds his security in a liberal standard of conduct, who doesn't believe in the resurrection from being spiritually dead and who doesn't accept that God has power for him to overcome sin. Is it possible today to join those who discard their belief in the judgment and who are selective as to which of the inspired writings they will accept? Is it possible to hold a theory of righteousness by faith in Jesus when it comes to justification, but to reject the righteousness by faith that is worked out in the life, in favor of trying hard in your own strength?

Whether you find yourself a Pharisee or Sadducee today, the picture looks pretty black. It looks like bad news right down the line. But there is good news for the Pharisees and Sadducees of today, just as there was good news for the Pharisees and Sadducees in the days of Jesus.

Jesus loves Pharisees too!

The good news for Pharisees and Sadducees is that they are loved by Jesus just as much as every other sinner in this world. "While Jesus ministered to all who came to Him, He yearned to bless those who came not. While He drew the publicans, the heathen,

71

and the Samaritans, He longed to reach the priests and teachers who were shut in by prejudice and tradition. He left untried no means by which they might be reached."—*The Desire of Ages*, p. 265. Christ is able to save Pharisees and Sadducees and all of the people who have been followers of these leaders and have partaken of their spirit. Jesus is still seeking to bring each one to know Him personally, to come to Him personally, and to accept personally His gift of salvation.

What is the good news for the Pharisees? The good news is that being a Pharisee is not the unpardonable sin. The disease of hypocrisy is not incurable. Jesus has the power available to change even the Pharisee and Sadducee so that they are righteous inwardly as well as outwardly. You can join the exceptions to the rule. You might join one of the leading Pharisees who came for a nighttime visit with Jesus to discuss the subject of religion, but who went away to experience the new birth that Jesus told him of in their interview. He found the vital relationship with God and gave of his riches to support the early church after the crucifixion of Jesus.

You might join a man named Simon, who held a feast to pay Jesus back for healing him of his leprosy. But he ended up accepting Jesus at his own feast and became a follower of Christ.

You can join the friendly scribe who came to Jesus for the purpose of trapping Him and humiliating Him before the people, but who saw in Jesus' words a wisdom beyond his own. And Jesus said to him, "Thou art not far from the kingdom of God." Mark 12:34.

At the end of Jesus' ministry here on earth, when the Pharisees and Sadducees had finally united in their enmity against Him, the Sanhedrin was gathered together to determine how to rid themselves of this Jesus. And after the discussions had continued for some time, Caiaphas rose to his feet. With a sneer on his face, he said to the leaders who were assembled there, "Ye know nothing at all, nor consider that it is expedient for us, that one man should die for the people, and that the whole nation perish not. And this spake he not of himself: but being high priest that year, he prophesied that Jesus should die for that nation; and not for that nation only, but that he also should gather together in one the children of God that were scattered abroad." John 11:49-52.

That's the good news for Pharisees in one line—It is expedient for you that one man should die for the people. Listen, friendly scribe who comes to ply Jesus with questions, It is expedient for you that one man should die for the people. Listen, Nicodemus, who comes under cover of darkness, It is expedient for you that one man should die for the people. Listen, Simon, the leper, It is expedient for you that one man should die for the people. Listen, Pharisee, Sadducee, wherever you are today. You can give up on the double life, give up your external performance covering your inner emptiness, and come to Jesus for the free gift of salvation. It is expedient for you, it is good news for you, that one Man should die for the people. And one Man did die. Ever since that time, it has been good news. If you're playing follow-the-leader, you'll miss the good news. But you can be an exception and follow Jesus today.

The Good News About the Shaking

Did you know that God would rather have you out in the world, not even making a profession of Christianity, than have you in the church, but not fully committed to Him? *God would rather have people cold than lukewarm.* That's what the Bible teaches in Revelation 3:14-22. Jesus Himself is speaking, for it says in verse 14, "These things saith the Amen, the faithful and true witness, the beginning of the creation of God"—that's Jesus. Revelation is Jesus' own book, the only book in the Bible that begins by saying, "The Revelation of Jesus Christ." So it is Jesus Himself who says, verse 15, "I know thy works, that thou art neither cold nor hot: I would thou wert cold or hot." He prefers cold to lukewarm.

Jesus is talking here to the last of the seven churches, the church that exists until just shortly before Jesus comes. It's the church called Laodicea. Laodicea is known for its lukewarm condition, and because of its lukewarmness, God says, "So then because thou art lukewarm, and neither cold nor hot, I will spue thee out of my mouth." Verse 16. What is God saying here about lukewarm people? They make Him sick. Now of course God loves lukewarm people—but they still make Him sick. "Your self-righteousness is nauseating to the Lord Jesus Christ.''—Ellen G. White Comments, *S.D.A. Bible Commentary*, vol. 7, p. 963.

He says, ''Because thou art lukewarm, and neither cold nor hot, I will spue thee out of my mouth. Because thou sayest, I am rich, and increased with goods, and have need of nothing; and knowest not that thou art wretched, and miserable, and poor, and blind, and naked.'' Verses 16, 17. You'll have to admit that this rebuke to Laodicea is pretty hard-hitting. In order to understand more clearly what is at stake here, let's consider what it takes to make Laodicea.

Laodicea is lukewarm. In order for a church to be called Laodicea, or lukewarm, more than half of the people in Laodicea would have to be lukewarm, wouldn't they? If more than half of the people were other than lukewarm, then the church would have been described by another title. So you're going to find a lot of lukewarm people in Laodicea.

Lukewarm = Hot + Cold

What is lukewarm? Well, if you want lukewarm water from your kitchen faucet, you turn the hot water on partway and the cold water on partway, and you get lukewarm water. The cold-water control handle is usually on the right, and the hot-water control handle is usually on the left. That analogy helps us somewhat, because it reminds us that lukewarm is partly hot and partly cold. But it wouldn't make much sense to try to visualize a Christian who was hot on the left side and cold on the right side. So let's look in Matthew 23, letting the Bible interpret itself, to discover how a person can be partly hot and partly cold.

Please read the entire chapter of Matthew 23 on your own; we won't quote it here. But it contains one of Jesus's sternest rebukes to the religious leaders of His day. The central point of His rebuke was that they were like whited sepulchers. They looked good on the outside, but the inside was a mess. And Jesus called them hypocrites because of this.

The whited sepulchers of which Jesus spoke were white because the Jewish people would go out every year to the cemetaries, on their memorial day, and paint the tombs of the prophets. And as they painted the tombs of the prophets, they would say, "Isn't it a terrible thing that our fathers did to these lovely prophets?" And they'd splash on some more whitewash. When they had finally emptied their buckets, they would head back to Jerusalem, where they would plan the crucifixion of Jesus.

No matter how much they fixed up the outside of the sepulchers, the inside remained the same. And no matter how much they worked on the outside of their own lives, the inside was unchanged. This gives us a clue as to what makes a lukewarm person. A lukewarm person one who is hot on the outside, but cold on the inside. It's the kind of person who knows all the rules and regulations, who has beaten a hard path from his home to the church door, who knows all the forms and ceremonies, but who still keeps God at arm's length. The Laodicean is one who wouldn't think of doing anything wrong, who is trying to get to heaven by his good works, and who is so busy being good that he doesn't have time day by day to spend with God in His Word and in prayer. Recent surveys of church members indicate that about 80 percent of the church members today fit that description. Four out of five church members are not spending even five minutes a day developing a relationship with Jesus. And if I find myself in that situation, then it doesn't matter how long I've had my name on the church books or how many good deeds I perform or how much money I give into the church treasury. I'm still not a Christian, because a Christian is one who knows Jesus as his personal

Saviour and Friend. If I find myself in that position, then I am lukewarm—and God would prefer that I be completely cold instead!

It says in Revelation 3 that the lukewarm person is wretched and miserable and poor and blind and naked. Verse 17. And the reason that God would prefer that such a person was cold instead of lukewarm is because the one who is cold can be brought more easily to understand his need. The tragedy of the lukewarm church member is that although he is wretched and miserable and all the rest of it, *he doesn't know it*. That's what makes his condition so serious.

If you sleep, you'll die!

When a person is caught out in freezing weather, at first he feels the cold intensely. But after a time, as he begins to grow numb, it doesn't seem as cold as it did at first. The temptation comes to simply curl up somewhere and go to sleep. There comes a false sense of security—an impression of warmth where there is no warmth. But if you've heard about this or read about this from someone who has experienced the danger, you realize that there's no way you should give in to the temptation to go to sleep. You keep walking. You use every ounce of willpower and self-discipline to keep moving. You know if you stop, you'll die.

In the Christian life, the temptation comes to depend upon good behavior and moral living instead of to depend upon Jesus. It's easy to neglect the relationship with Christ. At times the temptation is almost overpowering to give up the struggle to make time to spend seeking Him day by day, and just to sleep in every morning. But when you realize that this is where the battle in the Christian life is centered, you know you don't dare go to sleep and neglect the time of communion with God. You use every ounce of willpower and self-discipline to keep sacred that thoughtful hour for contemplating the life of Christ. And no matter how great the temptation to sleep in and forget about the relationship with Christ, *you know you'll die if you do*.

No matter how hot he is on the outside, the Laodicean who is cold on the inside is freezing to death. But he doesn't know it. He feels secure. That's why even cold people, who are aware that they are cold, have an advantage. They seek help. But the hard-hitting rebuke to the Laodicean is a desperate attempt on the part of a loving God to wake them up before they freeze to death spiritually.

However, the message to the Laodiceans is divided into two parts. God doesn't give rebukes without offering counsel. He doesn't point out our sins and problems just to make us feel hopeless. He has a solution. The second part of the message to the Laodicean church is the counsel to the lukewarm. "I counsel thee to buy of me gold tried in the fire, that thou mayest be rich: and white raiment, that thou mayest be clothed, and that the shame of thy nakedness do not appear; and anoint thine eyes with eyesalve, that thou mayest see. As many as I love, I rebuke and chasten: be zealous therefore, and repent." Verses 18, 19.

Perhaps we could paraphrase it this way: I counsel thee to buy of me faith and love, that thou mayest be rich; and the righteousness of Christ, that thou mayest be clothed and that the shame of thy nakedness do not appear; and anoint thine eyes with the Holy Spirit, that thou mayest see.

This counsel is God's answer to the problem of lukewarmness. The rebuke describes the problem and gives the solution to the problem.

Lukewarm people disappear

When Jesus actually does come back, there are going to be no lukewarm people. There are going to be only two classes of people, and they are described in

Scripture in various ways. They are called the good and the bad, the righteous and the wicked, the sheep and the goats, the wheat and the tares, the wise and the foolish, the hot and the cold. There are many different lables for them, but only two groups, Jesus said, "Behold, I come quickly; and my reward is with me, to give every man." Revelation 22:12. But there are only two rewards. There is no such thing as a lukewarm lake of fire for the lukewarm.

What happens to the lukewarm before Jesus comes? Where do they go? There are only two places for them to go—they go either hot or cold. Lukewarmness disappears before Jesus comes. Before He comes again, the fence straddlers disappear. There's no more middle of the road. Either you're going to be 100 percent solid in your relationship with Jesus, or you will have abandoned Him altogether. Jesus made it very clear that the dividing line between the hot and cold will be the relationship with Him. In Matthew 7, He said that not every one who says to Him, "Lord, Lord," will be in His kingdom. Even if they prophesy and cast out devils, and all the rest of it, He's going to say, "I never *knew* you: depart from me." Verses 21-23. John 17:3 says that knowing Jesus is what life eternal is all about. The two groups at the end will be those who don't know God and those who do know God. Personally. One-to-one. Now it so happens that this relationship is going to have a tremendous influence upon the performance and behavior of the person, including his relationship to the commandments of God, the Sabbath commandment, and all the rest of them. But the determining factor is whether or not the individual knows God for himself.

Something happens at the very end, just before Jesus comes, to cause the large middle group of lukewarm church members to disappear. There is a chapter telling of this time in a little book called *Early*

Writings, beginning on page 269. But it gives in detail exactly what happens experientially with God's people between now and when He comes again. It starts with what is called the "shaking."

The shaking

"I saw some, with strong faith and agonizing cries, pleading with God. Their countenances were pale and marked with deep anxiety, expressive of their internal struggle." Wait a minute! Does this mean that it's possible to have strong faith and internal struggles and deep anxiety all at the same time? That is good news! I can't tell you how much courage that brought to me when I first understood that. Because I've had my share of deep anxiety and internal struggles, and there was a time when I thought that anxiety and struggle proved that I was lacking in faith. No, you can have strong faith and deep anxiety at the same time. "Now and then their faces would light up with the marks of God's approbation." When? All the time? No, only now and then. "And again the same solemn, earnest, anxious look would settle upon them."

"Evil angels crowded around, pressing darkness upon them to shut out Jesus from their view, that their eyes might be drawn to the darkness that surrounded them, and thus they be led to distrust God and murmur against Him. Their only safety was in keeping their eyes directed upward." Notice the purpose of the evil angels. They wanted to shut out *Jesus* from the view of those who were praying. "As the praying ones continued their earnest cries, *at times* a ray of light from Jesus came to them, to encourage their hearts and light up their countenances." Here you have a group of people who are desperately concerned about something, to the point of pale faces, perspiration, deep anxiety, and internal struggles. Why are they anxious? If you check the context of this chapter for yourself, you'll discover that they haven't gotten the victory yet.

Now we see a second group. "Some, I saw, did not participate in this work of agonizing and pleading. They seemed indifferent and careless. They were not resisting the darkness around them, and it shut them in like a thick cloud. The angels of God left these and went to the aid of the earnest, praying ones. I saw angels of God hasten to the assistance of all who were struggling with all their power to resist the evil angels and trying to help themselves by calling upon God with perseverance. But His angels left those who made no effort to help themselves, and I lost sight of them." Notice what it is that the effort to help themselves involved: They endeavored to help themselves *by calling upon God*.

So here is the description of the two groups that emerge at the very end, and then the explanation of what causes the division. "I asked the meaning of the shaking I had seen and was shown that it would be caused by the straight testimony called forth by the *counsel* of the True Witness to the Laodiceans. This will have its effect upon the heart of the receiver, and will lead him to exalt the standard [Jesus] and pour forth the straight truth. Some will not bear this straight testimony. They will rise up against it, and this is what will cause a shaking among God's people."—Pages 69, 70, emphasis added. What causes the shaking? It's "the straight testimony called forth by the *counsel* of the True Witness to the Laodiceans."

Remember the two parts of the message to the church of Laodicea? First comes the rebuke. Then follows the "straight testimony called forth by the counsel," We wouldn't be surprised, perhaps, if the church was shaken up over the rebuke. We've seen people divided by stern rebukes before. But what is there about the "straight testimony called forth by the counsel," the reminder of the need for faith and love

81

and the righteousness of Christ and the Holy Spirit that shakes people up? How could anyone get shaken up over the need for faith, love, and righteousness of Christ?

It's a message to the heart

The counsel of the True Witness is not merely dealing with external standards, important as it is to maintain church standards. But it is possible to maintain high standards of behavior and live up to certain rules and regulations in the church and still have a heart far from Jesus. The True Witness has a message to the heart, for if the heart becomes a dwelling place for the Lord Jesus, if His righteousness is accepted within, the standards of behavior will follow. The only reason why people get shaken up over the message to the heart is that they have been finding their security in external righteousness. It happened in the days of Christ's first advent. The essence of Jesus' teaching was self-surrender. But that was an insult and an affront to the religious people who had been depending upon their own righteousness. So the great revival that is coming in the church (and I think we're on the verge of it today) is not going to be based upon the confession of heinous sins. It's going to be based upon coming to the realization that we have been living our "spotless" lives apart from Jesus. We will go to our knees and ask His forgiveness for leaving Him outside of our lives; and when He knocks at the door, we will respond, "Please, Lord, come in." That's what the revival is going to be all about.

The problem of the Laodiceans is not that they are short on works. The problem of the Laodiceans is that they have left Jesus standing out in the cold, knocking, asking for admission. And the revival that comes will be when they realize their undone condition and again admit Him into their hearts and lives.

After the shaking

The time of shaking is represented by the old-fashioned method of threshing grain. After the chaff was rubbed off the grain, it was sometimes placed in a large, flat basket. The grain-chaff mixture was tossed into the air. The wind would blow away the chaff, while the wheat fell back into the basket. The time of shaking we have just described is in a profoundly spiritual sense what has separated the true follower of Christ from the false.

The shaking time, both within and outside the church, leaves only four groups in the world:

Group 1. Knows God. Also knows about the three angels.

Group 2. Does not know God. Does know about the three angels.

Group 3. Knows God. But does not know about the three angels.

Group 4. Does not know God. Does not know about the three angels.

Groups 1 and 2 will be within the remnant church. Groups 3 and 4 will be outside the remnant church. When the time of the shaking is over, the time of the sifting will begin.

The members of the first group, who have been pleading with God and experiencing the deep anxiety and internal struggles, will have finally come to understand something that they had missed before, and they will have obtained the victory. They will have become overcomers. With their faces lighted up, with praise to God on their lips, and with the Holy Spirit in their hearts, they go from house to house proclaiming the good news. The people in the third group, who have known what it means to have a personal relationship with God, but who haven't understood the messages of the three angels and all that they represent, will begin joining with the remnant church. And the people in Group 4, who don't know God, who don't care to know Him, and who aren't interested in learning about the three angels either, will begin to get nervous. Just as it was in the days of Christ's first advent, they will be the ones who are the most "religious," both within and without the remnant church, who will be the most upset by the revival and reformation and victory that come from the relationship with Christ. And they will begin to do everything they possibly can to stop the great movement of God's people.

As the persecution begins and those in Group 4 begin to do their ugly work, the ones in Group 2 will leave the remnant church. Trying to avoid persecution, they will join Group 4 to become some of the bitterest enemies of those who remain in the remnant church. But as the trouble increases, the people who know God and who also know about the three angels will stay on their knees and continue to draw closer and closer to God.

When the sifting time has come to an end, the four groups look like this:

Group 1 and Group 3. Both know God, and both know about the three angels.

Group 2. Doesn't know God, but still remembers about the three angels.

Group 4. Doesn't know God, doesn't know about the three angels.

When the sifting time has ended, the final events will come on rapidly. The people in Group 2 can't quite forget about the charts on the closet doors and the things they learned before they left the remnant church. When the end begins to look like it's about here, they will say, It looks like the end; we'd better catch the last trolly out. But to their dismay they will find that the last trolly has left a long time ago. And they will begin to go from sea to sea and from coast to coast seeking the word of the Lord, but they won't find it. It will be too late.

The shaking and sifting time will be an awesome time to be alive. We are seeing it begin even now. It's one of the signs of the end that makes the sun, moon, and stars look like antiques. It is bad news for the ones who are being shaken out. It's bad news to see perhaps some of your closest friends grow colder and colder and finally leave altogether. But it's good news to see those who have known Jesus personally, but who have never learned about the doctrinal remnant, come in and take their places. And it's good news that when the times of the shaking and sifting have come, the coming of Jesus will almost be here.

It's happening today, my friend. People in the world, people in the church, are going *fast,* one way or the other.

He's still knocking

You still have a choice today to let Him in. Jesus is still saying to each one today, "Behold, I stand at the door, and knock: if any man hear my voice, and open the door, I will come in to him, and will sup with him, and he with me." Revelation 3:20. When Jesus knocks at the door of my heart, I don't want to be in the family room watching "Dallas." I don't want to be in the kitchen stuffing myself. I don't want to be upstairs listening to rock on my radio. I don't want to be out in the garage polishing my Mercedes. When Jesus knocks at the door, I want to be there to answer it, don't you?

We can be thankful today for His rebuke that wakes us up from our lethargy, and for His counsel that gives us courage and guidance. The time of the shaking is a time of good news, because God has done, and is doing, everything possible to help us to be shaken *in*, instead of shaken out. And the fellowship with Himself that He offers us is designed to last for an eternity if we invite Him into our hearts today.

The Good News About the Atonement

"For if, when we were enemies, we were reconciled to God by the death of his Son, much more, being reconciled, we shall be saved by his life. And not only so, but we also joy in God through our Lord Jesus Christ, by whom we have now received the atonement." Romans 5:10, 11. If you are interested in reading everything about the atonement, *per se*, in the New Testament, you just did! This verse in Romans is the only verse in the New Testament that mentions the atonement directly. It sounds as though the atonement is complete—"we have now received the atonement." Do you believe in a complete atonement? Or do you believe in an incomplete atonement? Or are you busy trying to remember what the word *atonement* means, anyway?

The *atonement* is a theological term, the kind of thing you might spend weeks or months studying at the seminary. But the evangelical Christians have sometimes charged us with not believing in a complete atonement, and the discussions and dialogue within our own church as to what we believe about the atonement have made it a very pertinent topic for today.

Perhaps the first thing we should do is get a good, clear definition of what the word *atonement* means. Of course, it is a combination of the words, "at one-ment." In the *Dictionary of Christian Theology* by Richardson, atonement is defined as follows: "To un-do the consequences of a wrong act with a view to the restoration of the relationship broken by the wrong act." What was the wrong act? It was the entrance of sin back there in the garden. Notice the key words, "with a view to the *restoration* of the *relationship* broken by the wrong act." What was the relationship that was broken by sin? It was a relationship where mankind was able to walk in the garden, in the cool of the day, and talk to God face-to-face. We don't have that kind of relationship with God today. So is the atonement complete, or not?

Complete, but not completed

At the General Conference session in Dallas, delegates were having a heavy discussion on the floor of the convention concerning the statement of beliefs of our church. They talked about the atonement, and finally, W. G. C. Murdock, who was the dean of our theological seminary for years, went to the micro-phone. He said, "Seventh-day Adventists have always believed in a complete atonement that is not com-pleted."

There is a sense in which the atonement must be complete, must have been complete at the cross. But there is also a sense in which the atonement is not yet completed. The evangelical Christian world wants to make sure that what Jesus did at the cross, when He took our place, is sufficient and enough. And it is true that His *sacrifice* was complete. But the atonement in-volves more than the sacrifice of Jesus in terms of undoing the consequences of the wrong act, in terms of restoring the relationship broken by the wrong act. For if the *atonement* had been completed at the cross, then there should have been no more sin or sickness or pain or sorrow or separation or battered children or hospitals or funeral trains or tombstones or broken hearts ever since.

We cannot add anything to what Jesus has already done for us. When Jesus died for our sins, according to the Scriptures, it was enough to purchase our salvation. All we can do is accept it. But although there is nothing that *we* can add to what Christ did at the cross, this does not mean that there is nothing that *He* can add to it! The process of redemption, the restoration of the broken relationship, was not completed at the cross. The Holy Spirit's work is essential to the restoration process, for without the work of the Spirit in our lives, we would be unable to accept the sacrifice of Jesus in our behalf. The work of Christ as our High Priest is essential to the restoration of the broken relationship. Without His priestly ministration, the restoration would be incomplete. And it is essential to the restoration of the broken relationship that He come again, to cleanse the world of sin and to vindicate His name and His law before the entire universe. There is far more involved in the atonement, there is far more involved in the restoration of the broken relationship between God and man, than the sacrifice of Jesus, essential as that sacrifice was to the plan of salvation.

The Day of Atonement

To understand more clearly what is involved in the atonement, let's go back to the Old Testament to examine the roots of the atonement concept. The book of Leviticus talks about a *day* of atonement, Leviticus 23:26-28. I would invite you to do your homework—look up each of these passages for yourself. Leviticus 16:8-10 tells about the two goats that Aaron cast lots over, at the beginning of the Day of Atonement. One of them was the Lord's goat, and the other was the scapegoat. Some have made the charge that we have made

Satan our Saviour by getting the scapegoat mixed up in the atonement. But there's nothing more biblical than the idea of the scapegoat being involved in the atonement. It's stated clearly in Leviticus 16:8-10. Read it for yourself.

Leviticus 16:15, 16 clearly says that the priest made the atonement. The goat did not make the atonement! There were two factors involved in the atonement—an animal and a priest who offered the sacrifice. So the work of the priest is essential to the atonement. And finally, in Leviticus 16:21, 22, comes the completion of the Day of Atonement with the scapegoat, representing the devil, sent into the wilderness never to be seen again. So the atonement services in ancient Israel included the whole day. When the sacrifice was offered in the courtyard, as a burnt offering, at the beginning of the day, the Day of Atonement was not yet completed. The sacrifice was complete. But the Day of Atonement was not completed. It was not until the scapegoat was sent away into the wilderness that the Day of Atonement was completed.

The good news of the complete sacrifice

The completeness of the atonement sacrifice is good news. Paul said, God "hath made him [Jesus] to be sin for us, who knew no sin; that we might be made the righteousness of God in him." 2 Corinthians 5:21. Because of the completeness of the sacrifice of the atonement, Jesus can come to you personally, today, and look at you with His friendly eyes. He can come to you with the good news that He will take all of your sins and give you all of His righteousness. He offers this today. Are you interested?

Perhaps you say, "That's what Jesus did for me twenty years ago, when I first became a Christian. But there's been a lot of water under the bridge since then. I've failed and fallen and sinned, again and again. I used up my 490 times of forgiveness long ago."

But there's good news for you too. Because of the complete sacrifice of the atonement, that verse is just as good for you today as when you first became a Christian. Jesus is still offering to you *today*, no matter who you are or where you've been, His righteousness in exchange for your sin. You can accept this again today, and again stand before God, more than just plain forgiven—super forgiven! For you can stand before God as though you had never ever even sinned. Jesus *did* pay it all, and it has been good news for our world, and for our universe, ever since.

It is also good news that the complete atonement is not yet completed! It's good news for Lloyd Funkhouser, who was a member of my parish. You may have read the book *Funky*, the story of his life written by Barbara Herrera. He lost both of his legs as the result of an automobile accident. I've seen him teach the Sabbath School lesson from his wheelchair. I've seen him on the platform in his wheelchair, singing for special music, "I need Thee, precious Jesus, for I am very poor; / a stranger and a pilgrim, I have no earthly store. / I need the love of Jesus to cheer me on my way, / to guide my doubting footsteps, to be my strength and stay." If the *atonement* is completed, the news is bad for Lloyd Funkhouser. Because he's been looking forward to a day when he can run and jump and leap like a deer. We're going to run the 100-yard dash with him one day and rejoice to see him win.

It's good news that the complete atonement is not yet completed. It's good news for Eldene Childs, who lies in a nursing home year after weary year. She is paralyzed from the neck down. It would be bad news for her if the *atonement* were completed, for she is looking forward to being able to feed herself, dress herself, and move freely wherever she wants to go. She may never want to lie down again for all of eternity!

I read a newspaper account of a man in California who beat his little six-year-old daughter. She wouldn't cry. So he kept beating her for half an hour. At the end of half an hour, she asked, "Daddy, can I please have a drink of water?" And then she died. It would have never happened if the atonement were completed.

You can walk down the streets of Bombay, India, over the bodies of sleeping people who find on the streets their only home. Father, mother, children, and grandmother—all there together, starving to death. It would never happen if the atonement were completed.

The sin and suffering and sorrow go on. It would be bad news if the atonement were completed and there was nothing more to be offered. Yet we are given the good news, the hope, the promise, that the time will come when the atonement *will* be completed, and the entire universe will be freed from the tragedy of sin.

The good news for today is that the atonement's completion is nearly upon us. We don't have much longer to wait. Revelation assures us that the hour of God's judgment is come. That really is what the whole business of the Day of Atonement is about! We rejoice, because we realize that our earthly custody is about over. Jesus, our Substitute and Saviour, our High Priest and Intercessor, our Judge and our King, has almost finished His work. The atonement is soon to be completed.

Because of this tremendous truth, all of the details of the final events become good news as well, for each one is an additional step closer to the time when the atonement will at long last be completed and the restoration of the broken relationship will be complete. In conclusion I'd like to share a parable to illustrate the fact that the atonement, while not yet completed, is fast approaching completion. And that's *good* news!

Good news and bad news

Tom was a criminal—a really bad one—not just your ordinary, everyday, small-town crook. He was big-time. He was a cheat, liar, robber, gambler, adulterer, and murderer. He would sell his own mother if he thought it could get him what he wanted. He prided himself on having no scruples, on having done everything there was to do. But he had been caught.

Now he sat in prison trying to figure out what his next move would be. He thought desperately of escape. He thought of suicide. Neither was possible. He was too closely guarded. He practiced all sorts of speeches denying his illegal activities, but none of them sounded convincing, even to him. He was in big trouble, and Tom knew it. The longer he sat there, forced to think, the more despondent he became. The whole future looked black. It seemed that things couldn't possibly be worse. He was really at the end of his rope.

Then one day a prison official came to Tom's cell and said, "Tom, we have some good news for you and some bad news." Tom looked up sullenly. Yet deep inside he felt eager for any change in the misery of just sitting there day after day, helpless. He braced himself for the worst. "The good news is that a lawyer has been assigned to your case, and he is the best lawyer in the whole world." Tom was silent. He knew there was a catch somewhere. And sure enough, there was. The official continued, "The bad news is that the prosecuting attorney has also been assigned, and he's the best prosecuting attorney in the whole world." Tom remained silent. The prison official shook his head. "The laywer must be crazy to think of defending you. But anyhow, he'll be in to see you tomorrow." And he turned and walked away.

The next day, a quiet sort of gentleman came to

Tom's cell and knocked. Tom looked up startled and then laughed bitterly. "You've got the key, man," he said. "Why knock?"

"I only go where I'm invited," replied the visitor.

"Well, come on in," Tom said. "I wasn't going anywhere."

The visitor opened the door, entered, and sat down.

"So who are you, anyhow?" Tom asked.

"I'm a lawyer. I understand you're looking for a lawyer to take your case."

"Yes," said Tom. "It's about time they finally sent me someone. But tell me about your qualifications. The man here said you're supposed to be good. But if you're so good, I may not be able to pay your price. Level with me so I can know what to expect."

"Well," said the lawyer, "I have some good news for you and some bad news. The good news is that I have never lost a case. I can guarantee the outcome of the trial, if you'll place yourself in my hands."

"And the bad news is the price, right?" said Tom. The lawyer nodded.

"OK, lay it on me. How much is it going to cost?"

"It's free."

"I beg your pardon?"

"It's free," the lawyer repeated.

"Hey, I'm not a rich man, but I don't need your charity," said Tom stiffly. "If I can just get out of this dump, I can raise the money."

All of the atonement is a gift!

The lawyer smiled kindly. "No, if you want my help, you must accept it as a gift. You cannot pay me for any part of it. It is totally and completely free. It's one of the conditions for my taking your case."

Tom was silent for a few minutes and then asked,

"What are the other conditions for receiving your help?"

"Well," the lawyer replied, "I have some more good news and bad news for you. The good news is that all you have to do, if you want me to take your case, is just ask me. And I'll take it immediately. The bad news is that if I take your case, you'll have to plead guilty."

Tom gasped.

"Aren't you guilty?" asked the lawyer.

"Uh, yes. But if I plead guilty to all the charges made against me, I won't have a ghost of a chance. They'll throw the book at me. How can you possibly think you'll be able to help me if I plead guilty?"

"I have some bad news for you and some good news," said the lawyer. "The bad news is that if you plead guilty, of course you'll be convicted. And if you don't plead guilty, the prosecuting attorney has sufficient proof that you'll be convicted anyway. Either way, there's no doubt but that you will get the death sentence."

"Then why even have a trial?" said Tom.

"You've forgotten that I have some good news," said the lawyer. "I am willing to take your sentence and let you go free."

"No way," cried Tom. "You aren't the one who has lived the rotten life. I'm the one. I've done nothing good. I don't deserve anything but death. Hanging's too good for me. There's no way I could let you pay for my crimes."

The lawyer replied gently, "But, Tom, I already have paid. All that remains is for you to accept my substitution in your behalf. It is yours, if you accept it, and it's complete. It will cover completely for your crimes."

After a long moment, Tom asked quietly, "Is there anything else I should know before the trial?"

The lawyer nodded. "Yes, I have some good news for you and some bad news. The good news is that you *will* be pardoned. There's no question about that. You'll be able to stand before God and man as though you had never even sinned. But there may be some bad news for you."

"What's that?" asked Tom.

"It's this—you won't be a criminal anymore."

"What do you mean?"

"You will be a new person. You'll have a new direction. There is more to my work than simply paying the penalty for your misdeeds. I have even more to complete in your life. While you are waiting for your trial to take place, you won't continue to lie and cheat and steal and kill. You will become pure and honest and trustworthy. We will work together closely, you and I. We'll become good friends. As we associate together day by day, you will come to hate the things you once loved, and love the things you once hated. You will become a new person altogether."

"I'm not so sure about that," said Tom. "The prospect of pardon looks pretty good to me, but what if I want to go my own way? Can't we just arrange it so I can be released from the penalty of my actions? Isn't that complete enough? Do I really have to stop being a crook?"

"The pardon is only good for those who are willing for me to give them a new life," said the lawyer.

Tom stared at the floor while the lawyer waited patiently for his decision. At last Tom raised his head. "I would like to ask you to take my case," he said. "I admit that I'm guilty. And I really don't want to keep on being a crook. I accept your help." The lawyer rose and held out his hand. Tom took it firmly, and the contract was sealed.

"Is there anything else I should know before you leave?"

But still the atonement is not completed!

"Yes, there's one final thing," replied the lawyer. "I have one last bit of good news and bad news for you."

Tom smiled. "Give me the bad news first and get it over with. Although all of a sudden it doesn't seem as though any of your bad news has been that bad!"

The lawyer smiled, too. "All right. The bad news is that we have set the date for your trial."

"Why, that's not bad news at all," exclaimed Tom. "With a lawyer like you, do you think I would want to stay here in this place forever and never even have my case go to court? The news of the coming judgment is terrific news! And your good news had better be pretty good to outdo that."

The lawyer looked into Tom's eyes for a moment before he said gently, "The good news is this: When you come to trial, I will not only be your lawyer. I will be your judge as well."